25

The Saturday Book

Twenty-fifth Year

The Saturday Book

EDITED BY JOHN HADFIELD

HUTCHINSON OF LONDON

THE SATURDAY BOOK was founded in 1941 by Leonard Russell and has been edited since 1952 by John Hadfield. This twenty-fifth annual issue has been made and printed in Great Britain by The Anchor Press, Ltd. and bound by William Brendon & Son Ltd., both of Tiptree, Essex.

The frontispiece reproduces a painting in gouache by John Tunnard, entitled 'Mirage', which was commissioned for THE SATURDAY BOOK

Introduction

FOR AN essentially miscellaneous annual such as *The Saturday Book* a quarter of a century seems an unbelievably long span of life. The survival in a competitive market-place for so long a period of a 'gift-book' which has no more specific aim than to entertain the eye and stimulate the curious mind is a seemingly unaccountable phenomenon.

Has any other miscellany matched our record? To find an answer to this question we turned back to the 'twenties and 'thirties of the nineteenth century. This was the golden age of the miscellaneous annual, when editors were men and women of literary and social distinction, and contributors included writers of the stature of Coleridge, Byron, Keats, Scott and Tennyson. As we expected, we found that our record had in fact been surpassed by the most famous of all, *The Keepsake*, which first appeared in 1827 and ran for thirty years. *The Keepsake*, however, had at least three changes of editor—two of them were Ladies of Title—whereas *The Saturday Book* has had only two editors—both commoners.

We can find no other competitor which has reached the quarter-century. One of the most distinguished, *The Literary Souvenir*, which was edited continuously by Alaric A. Watts, appeared for eleven years (1825–35). *Friendship's Offering, or The Annual Remembrancer*, which started in 1825 and ended in 1844, ran us closer than most.

The twentieth century offers few competitors. We recall with affection *The New Forget-me-Not* and *The New Keepsake*, both delightfully decorated by Rex Whistler, which appeared in the early nineteen-thirties; but they had no continuing life. That admirable rival (albeit a specialised one), *The Compleat Imbiber*, appears to be in good health, but has not yet notched a third of our score.

·≫ INTRODUCTION ≪·

Unkind critics may say that one reason for our longevity is that *The Saturday Book* does not concern itself with serious matters such as philosophy, politics and religion, and has always indulged in some frivolity. Well, we make no claims other than entertainment value for items such as Olive Cook's and Edwin Smith's pictorial documentation of the Bicycle in this issue, or for Charles Gibbs-Smith's annual expedition with scissors and paste in the Elysian fields of female ephemera. We recognise, too, that whereas *The Anniversary* of 1829 was grandly embellished with engravings after Turner and Landseer our issue of 1965 has the sauce to offer its readers a series of photographs taken by a London taxi-driver.

Still, the *Saturday* roll-call is by no means an undistinguished one, starting with Allingham (Margery), Bates, Betjeman, Church and De la Mare, and ending amongst the Sitwells, Waugh and Wodehouse. Several valuable books have developed out of articles in our pages. And, although we make no great claims to originality, we believe we have often (perhaps inadvertently) anticipated movements of taste.

It is perhaps in the field of taste and fashion that we take most pride in the *Saturday* record. We have never tried to follow fashion; indeed we have deliberately sought to investigate what is at the moment out of fashion, and rediscover or reassess the work of authors or artists whose talents, in our view, have been insufficiently recognised. Such a feature is that which Sir Herbert Read contributes to this year's issue. It gives us particular pleasure to print such a contribution as this.

Now to match the record of *The Keepsake!*

J.H.

For permission to reprint in this issue certain copyright poems acknowledgements are made to the following: Messrs John Baker Ltd., for poems by Lord Alfred Douglas and Olive Custance (Lady Alfred Douglas); the Bodley Head for a poem by John Gray; the Society of Authors as the literary representative of the estate of the late Sir William Watson; Messrs Heinemann for a poem by Arthur Symons; and Messrs Herbert Jenkins for two poems by Edmund John.

Contents

FIN

DE SIÈCLE

The Turn
of the Century

 SIMON NOWELL-SMITH

THE CALENDAR is an artefact, the arbitrary creation of Man. If the birth of Christ had been dated by Dionysius Exiguus fifty years earlier, the end of the nineteenth century would have coincided with the death of Wordsworth and the birth of Maupassant; if twenty-five years later, the twentieth century would have opened with the first collection of poems by T. S. Eliot and the birth of *The New Yorker*. There is nothing sacrosanct about 'the turn of a century'. Nevertheless the month of January, 1901, according to the Gregorian calendar which western Europe uses, was doubly significant in Britain. It marked the beginning of a new century and also the end of the reign of Queen Victoria, the longest reign in English history.

Between Wordsworth and Eliot, between *Bleak House* and *A Passage to India*, *The Ring* and *Wozzek*, the Pre-Raphaelite Brotherhood and the Surrealist Manifesto, between what is typically mid-nineteenth century and what we like to call 'modern', are great gulfs fixed. But gulfs, when you look into them, are often more apparent than real, and modernity is the most imprecise of concepts. Meredith's *Modern Love*, of almost exactly a hundred years ago, is much closer to our present ways of thinking than George Moore's *Modern Lover* of 1883, or than Galsworthy's *Modern Comedy* of 1929. At the turn of the century Meredith was an old man, George Moore in mid career, and Galsworthy had only just begun. All three represent bricks in the bridge over the gulf that separates older from newer ideas of morality. Yeats almost alone stands as a giant astride the gulf between older and newer modes of thought and of literary expression.

[9]

Yeats described himself as, in his youth, 'all Pre-Raphaelite'. He was flattered when William Morris told him, 'You write my sort of poetry.' He moved in his thirties in a coterie of writers and artists whose promise, for the most part, was not to be fulfilled. They formed the Rhymers' Club, and wrote and illustrated *The Yellow Book* and *The Savoy*; they sipped absinthe— *la sorcière glauque*—with Oscar Wilde, before the fall, at the Café Royal. Some, like Beardsley and Conder, Ernest Dowson, Lionel Johnson and Hubert Crackenthorpe, died young of drink or consumption, insanity or suicide. Others, like Ricketts and Shannon, Le Gallienne and Arthur Symons, persisted as minor artists and *littérateurs* well into the new century. Yet others deserted the muses for journalism (Robbie Ross), librarianship (Victor Plarr) or the Church (John Gray). (It was rarer for a parson, like Selwyn Image, to exchange the surplice for the smock.) These are among the men who are sometimes held up as representing the spirit of 'the 'nineties'. They regarded them- selves as *fin-de-siècle*, which after all was only an accident of the calendar; and they were regarded by their more robust contem- pories, not in every instance without justice, as decadent, or, as *Punch* preferred, 'daycadong'. Collectively—and I do not wish to be unfair to any one of them as individuals—the lesser luminaries of the period are portrayed, with satirical exaggeration of course, in Max Beerbohm's story of the imaginary Enoch Soames. Max was the least modern, and survives as at once the most detached, and the most 'dated', figure in the landscape. Soames was the author of two slim volumes, *Negations* and *Fungoids*; he called himself a 'Catholic Diabolist', and eventually rendered up his soul to the Devil. It is not irrelevant that Yeats, as well as Beardsley, was at one time a keen student of Diabolism.

With the end of the Victorian era time did not stand still, but writers and philosophers, painters and musicians, had a moment in which to take stock of where they stood, what they stood for, and where they wanted to go. 'Everybody', said Yeats, 'got down off his stilts; henceforth nobody drank absinthe with his black coffee; nobody went mad; nobody committed suicide; nobody joined the Catholic Church; or if they did I have forgotten.'

But there were other spirits abroad in the 'nineties, and had been for some time. Indeed the later Victorians had long been shaking off the trammels of early Victorianism. Consider for a moment the transition from the sober 'eighties to those naughty 'nineties. The first elementary education act had been passed in 1870. By the early 'eighties its products were reading *Tit-Bits*, or attending the new 'continuative' colleges which were to become the redbrick universities of a later day. Never had literature, good and bad, for the masses, literate and illiterate, been so plentiful, or so cheap. In higher education women were admitted, for the first time, to something approaching equality with men; they were practising as doctors; married women were granted the same rights to property as their unmarried sisters; the House of Commons even considered—only to reject it— an amendment to the Reform Bill of 1884 that 'words importing the masculine gender' should be interpreted as embracing the fair sex. In the field of science both domestic electric lighting and the petrol-driven motor-car were inventions of the 'eighties, though it was not until the next decade that the first petrol-omnibus was seen in London, or that the lights in the newly wired Grosvenor House went out at a *soirée*, only to come on again and reveal thirteen fearful ladies clinging to Mr. Henry James.

One of the most agreeable aspects of minor poetry and *belles-lettres* of the 'nineties was their physical presentation. The visual arts are dealt with elsewhere in this *Saturday Book*, but I must be allowed a brief glance at *Art Nouveau* in its literary context. Again, the roots are in the 'eighties, or earlier. Two influences had been at work to evolve the characteristic 'decorated'—as distinct from illustrated—books of the period. Charles Ricketts, the most distinguished book-designer in a period distinguished for the excellence of its book design, learnt most of what he knew from Rossetti; and it was Rossetti who, way back in the early 'sixties, had set a fashion for publishers of verse to have their bindings designed by real, rather than hack, artists.

The other influence, paradoxically, was William Morris. Morris's peculiar combination of medievalism and socialism led him into many strange paths: among other things it led him to believe that book-production should be a handicraft, pursued and executed by the hands of individual artists and craftsmen. The fashion for private-press books spilled over into commercial book-production, under the impetus of a new generation of publishers like Elkin Mathews and John Lane, who took infinite pains with title-pages, decorated or plain, with type-areas and margins, and with bindings; and these new publishers experimented with books of unusual, and often unpractical, shapes. *Art Nouveau* twined its tendrils round Yeats and Francis Thompson, John Davidson and Lord de Tabley; and if A. E. Housman, his own typographer, inclined to a severer taste, his brother Laurence made a reputation as a decorator of bindings and title-pages for Christina Rossetti and George Meredith long before his other reputation as a playwright.

Response to book illustration and book decoration is largely subjective. I personally find that the intricacies and irrelevances, and the warmth, of Laurence Housman and Althea Gyles help to make minor poetry readable, whereas the other characteristically ninetyish style, the hard, frigid line style of Beardsley and his imitators, alienates the sympathy that the poor poet so sadly needs.

Music also, seldom one of Britain's more flourishing arts— 'our *piano*, rather than our *forte*', as one wit put it—enjoyed a notable renascence in the 'eighties, leading in the 'nineties to Elgar's *Enigma Variations* and Henry Wood's promenade concerts at the Queen's Hall. The serious theatre, unlike the music hall, had been almost moribund in mid-century: neither Browning nor Tennyson could write durable plays. It was in the 'eighties that the theatre took on a new lease of life, under a diversity of *stimuli*.

On the one side, the side of the angels, was Henry Irving, the greatest of actor-managers, who took both the integrity of his art and the moral rectitude of his company *au grand sérieux*. Gladstone wished him to accept a knighthood, the first in the profession, in 1883, but Irving did not feel that he had earned it, by unconditional victory in his battle for respectability, until 1895. On the other side was Ibsen, a foreigner no doubt, but the theatre knows no frontiers. Ibsen's dramas had swept France and Germany before, with their revolutionary stagecraft and disturbing psychology, they profoundly shocked London audiences. The Independent Theatre, which finally established his reputation in England in 1891, went on to stage Bernard Shaw's first play, *Widowers' Houses*, in 1892.

Shaw, meanwhile, had been an explosive force from the beginning in the counsels of the Fabian Society (1884), and the Fabian Society, like the Society for Psychical Research (1882), was to help shape modes of thinking throughout the 'nineties and beyond. In fiction the rising star was Rudyard Kipling. There was no lack of vigour, nothing *fin-de-siècle*, about Kipling, a twenty-three-year-old who under an Indian sun could turn out seven paper-backs, containing seventy-seven short stories, in the course of a single year. (The other star in the firmament of fiction in that year, 1888, was Mrs. Humphry Ward. Her novels of religious doubt and social betterment in the early 'nineties outrivalled Kipling in point of sales; her name was bracketed in the best circles with those of Dickens and George Eliot and Hardy; and the titles of her books, with one exception, I challenge my readers to recall.) As a patriotic and vernacular ballad-monger from the 'eighties onwards Kipling revitalised an old tradition. He was to have many imitators, including Conan Doyle (Sherlock Holmes, incidentally, made his first bow in *A Study in Scarlet* in 1887, though his fame, like the *Strand Magazine* which fostered it, came later); and inevitably, in a sea-faring nation, the tradition was destined to find expression in the Newbolt of 'Drake's Drum' (1896) and in the *Salt-Water Ballads* (1902) of our present Poet Laureate.

Kipling has always been a controversial figure. Journalist, jingoist, popular story-writer and versifier, he was the supreme expression of one aspect of the turn of the century. The only historical event that precisely covers that turn is the Boer War, which lasted from 1899 to 1902. The Boer War aroused passionate emotions and demonstrations at home: friendships were broken, families divided, party loyalties abjured, over the issues of pacificism and pro-Boerism. But the war itself, fought by professional soldiers, not by the committed youth of a nation, was so much more remote from ordinary people's lives than the great world wars were to be, that it produced no comparable spate of novels and poetry, and no great novelist or poet. Kipling believed in the Empire, not 'right or wrong', but in spite of its warts. With sixty years' hindsight it is possible to judge that both those who extolled and those who condemned his imperialism at the time did him less than justice; and also that those who awarded him the Nobel Prize for literature in 1907 were no more, and no less, wrong-headed than those who since have pooh-poohed his claim to a niche in the literary Valhalla.

If the Boer War did not inspire great literature, neither did it inspire great painting, though the hope lingered on that it might. 'The illusion has been considerably shaken', wrote the editor of *The Year's Art* in 1900, 'that we cannot produce a school of battle-painters.' The Royal Academy's summer exhibition in the following year was dominated, apart from Sargent, by portraits in oil and marble of the late Queen, and representations of her funeral. The other great *genre* of the year was the stiff, sentimental scene of soldiers leaving for, or returning from, the field of battle; but, as *The Times* art critic remarked, with a nostalgic memory of the scarlet uniforms of older wars, 'undoubtedly khaki is a serious injury to the war painters'. What the war did inspire was the war correspondent and the black-and-white illustrator of the weekly news magazines. The camera seldom ventured within the sound of gun-fire before the 1914 war; but the standard of reporting and illustration was higher than it had ever been. The tradition of 'sketching' among regular army officers, by no means excluding Baden-Powell ('the hero of Mafeking') himself, was also exceptionaly high, and of considerable historical value.

*　　*　　*　　*　　*

Let us turn to the new books and plays that were available, in those four years of the Boer War, to the young people destined to become famous in the next literary generation. At twenty Virginia Woolf may already have been visited by the fancy that the Marlow of Conrad's *Lord Jim* took aboard with him Henry James's *The Wings of the Dove*; and E. M. Forster, at twenty-two, comparing James's *The Sacred Fount* with Wells's *Love and Mr. Lewisham*, may already have reached the decision that 'my own prejudices are with Wells'. We can imagine the precocious Joyce, who already at eighteen had published an essay on Ibsen, not only seeing Yeats's *Countess Cathleen* at Lady Gregory's theatre in Dublin, but perhaps importing Gide's *L'Immoraliste* from Paris. What is less easily imagined is that D. H. Lawrence should have sent for Freud's *Interpretation of Dreams*, in German, from Vienna: another decade was to pass before Englishmen became even dimly aware of Freud. Meanwhile, across the Atlantic, T. S. Eliot in his 'teens was surely reading William James's *Varieties of Religious Experience*. And Edith Sitwell, also in her 'teens? . . . perhaps, torn from the last poems of George Meredith or the first of Walter de la Mare in order to stand—not sit—to Sargent for his 'Sitwell Family', she was allowed to go, still in her long scarlet frock, to the first night of *Tosca* at Covent Garden. The still younger age-group that was to furnish the war poets of the First World War, like Wilfred Owen and Robert Graves, was still too young even for *Stalky and Co.* and Kathleen Nesbit's *Treasure Seekers*.

These at least were some of the books and plays that belong to the turn of the century, the last years of the old reign and the first of the new. But none of them marks a clear distinction between Victorian and Edwardian literature. We all know what we mean by Victorian literature. We mean giants and prophets, or men who were considered to be giants and prophets— Dickens and Thackeray, Tennyson and Browning, Carlyle and Ruskin and Matthew Arnold. We may include Meredith and Hardy, though it was only when he was nearing sixty, a little before the end of the century, that Hardy began to publish the poetry which represents his influence on more modern writers. But when we speak of Edwardian literature, and consider whether there is any literature that can be called characteristically Edwardian, we think not of giants but of novelists who wrote in an essentially Victorian tradition: Wells and Galsworthy and Arnold Bennett, men whose stature is diminished when seen through latter-day spectacles.

The nearest of these to the stature of prophet was Wells, but it was precisely in his imaginative writing that he was least, and least wished to be thought, a prophet. Time and the critics have dealt harshly with these three, though not with their contemporary, Joseph Conrad: but then Conrad stands outside any tradition. Time has all but obliterated such lesser Edwardians as Maurice Hewlett, Arthur Machen and Arthur Morrison, along with a host of once popular poets.

I have said that Yeats stands astride the gulf between the Victorian and the modern. I should perhaps have said that Robert Bridges does too—Bridges, whose best lyrics appeared in 1873, and his crowning achievement, *The Testament of Beauty*, in 1929: but I doubt whether the modern critic would award the bay of true modernity to that great poet. In any case, to call either Yeats or Bridges Edwardian would be to misuse the epithet. When the Edwardian revival sets in, and it is overdue, neither of these near-giants will need a leg-up to Parnassus.

The Case of John Singer Sargent

RICHARD ORMOND

IN HIS OWN TIME Sargent stood at the very pinnacle of artistic success, hailed on almost every side as one of the great masters of his age. His portraits, the show-pieces of successive Royal Academy exhibitions, were considered to be in the European tradition of grand portraiture, as well as being intensely modern in their vivid and brilliant technique. The *beau monde* of the Edwardian world flocked to his studio until in desperation Sargent wrote to Lady Radnor: 'Ask me to paint your gates, your fences, your barns, which I would gladly do, but *not the human face*' (1904).

By 1910 he had refused any further commissions for oil portraits, but his fame lived on, augmented now by his colourful and scintillating water-colours, his oil landscapes and his murals. Even the advanced New English Art Club advertised exhibitions with his magic name: 'Works by Mr. John Sargent and others . . .' In 1922 Asher Wertheimer bequeathed the great series of Wertheimer portraits by Sargent to the nation, and these hung for a time in the National Gallery, before Sir Joseph Duveen built a special Sargent Galley at the Tate Gallery to house them. At his death in 1925 Sargent was mourned by the whole country, and in the following year a memorial exhibition at the Royal Academy contained over six hundred of his works, perhaps the largest one-man show ever held up to that time.

But, as Sickert said, the only man to abstain from the Sargent boom was Sargent himself. Reserved and austere, with his imposing bulk and bulging eyes, he was only at ease with his family and close friends, detesting social occasions and the flattery of the fashionable world. His life was dedicated to his art, and his apparently mysterious private life held no real secrets beyond his easel and his paint-brush. Unlike Boldini or

Helleu or even de Laszlo, he did not revel in the society which he depicted, nor did he traffic in dazzling effects for their own sake, or the arbitrary and fashionable 'chic' of such painters. His aim was to make his hand express exactly what his eye saw, with the utmost economy and detachment, within the context of his ideas of style, and the limitations that portraiture necessarily entails. This devastating accuracy, and wonderful grasp of feature, never obscured by accessories or flourishes, led people to think that his portraits were social satires, or penetrating psychological studies. They were neither. Nor were they merely social documents, as some critics have described them, for the sense of human character and individuality is never lost. They represent exactly what Sargent saw in front of him, transformed into paint with an unselfconscious virtuosity and very real painterly power.

Because Sargent was the subject of so much exaggerated adulation, and because discerning critics could see that his work was very far from being 'the latest thing', he was attacked ferociously. The early part of this century was a time when the battle for and against modern art was very fierce, and Sargent, an artist of great stature, was an inevitable butt. He was, after all, one of the bastions of the Royal Academy, working in a representational, even academic, style. His name became firmly linked with the Edwardian world, and, to a succeeding generation, such a world appeared frivolous, superficial and not very admirable. Sargent's reputation suffered accordingly; he became pigeon-holed and forgotten, regarded as a social phenomenon, a brilliant executant, but not a real artist. It is only more recently that his artistic achievement has begun to be valued more fairly.

He was born in Florence in 1856, the son of American parents (he remained an American citizen all his life) who had decided to forego the material advantages of their own country in favour of European culture and a more sophisticated society. They wandered from one fashionable centre to another—Paris, London, Nice, Pau, Florence, Rome, Munich, Switzerland—an unsettled, migratory existence that was cosmopolitan, but cannot have been very satisfying. Mrs Sargent was the dominating force in the family, encouraging her son's love of drawing,

CARNATION, LILY, LILY, ROSE, 1887. *Tate Gallery*

MRS. WILTON PHIPPS, 1884. *Coll. Mrs. R. P. Grenfell*

GRAHAM ROBERTSON, oil sketch, 1894–5. *Private Collection*

literature and music. Sargent was well read in European literature, and a very competent pianist, who later helped many
struggling composers and musicians including Fauré, Grainger
and Loeffler. After studying art in Florence, and overcoming his
father's objections to his career as an artist, Sargent went to
Paris in 1874, and entered the studio of Carolus-Duran.

Carolus-Duran was an ebullient and dashing little man, who
had made his reputation as a portraitist with the exhibition of
his *La Femme au Gant* at the Salon of 1869. He was a passionate
admirer of Velasquez, teaching the importance of tone and half-
tone, and employing a dry, flat, low-toned technique, with
sparkling accents and high-lights. It was a style of great elegance
and vivid realism, and it influenced Sargent profoundly. There
were other influences too, for Sargent was friendly with Manet,
Monet, and others of the advanced French school; and their
influence is reflected in his early landscapes and subject pictures.

Much of his early work is experimental, bearing the signs of
his struggle with technique and composition, and also of his
artistic integrity and intelligence. An example of his portraiture,
at a time when he was breaking away from the influence of
Carolus-Duran and developing his mature style, is his portrait
of Mrs Wilton Phipps (page 20), painted in England in 1884. The
figure set against a dark background, the shimmering qualities
of light, the brilliant contrasts of black and white (in the wide-
boned waistband and bustle, in the black neckband and ribbons
against the white dress), the creamy flesh-tones, the single accent
of colour in the pink bouquet of flowers, all recall his debt to
French art and Manet in particular. The brushwork is much
richer and looser than Carolus-Duran's, though it lacks the
thick impasto of Sargent's later work, and the image is superbly
sophisticated and human too. The hands coming up to enclose
the ribbon and flowers are both tender and elegant, and provide
an entirely natural solution to a formal problem. The modelling
of the head shows that grasp of structure and tone (the lesson
had been well learnt from Velasquez and Franz Hals) which
were the keystones of all his portraits. It is not surprising that
Henry James wrote of the 'uncanny spectacle of a talent which
on the very threshold of its career has nothing more to learn'.

Such portraits had, from 1877, won him respect and admiration at the annual Salon exhibitions in Paris, but no great stream of clients. In 1884 he had pinned his hopes to his provocative portrait of the celebrated beauty Madame Gautreau, but for some unknown reason it raised a storm of abuse, and his new studio of the Boulevard Berthier remained empty. It was chiefly because of this that he decided to try his luck in England, where he already had some valuable patrons. But his early years there were not easy ones, and his brilliant Impressionist landscapes, which he painted at Broadway in Worcestershire (in company with Abbey, Millet, James, Gosse and others), did not bring in any money. His portraits were regarded as French, clever and revolutionary, and were severely criticised; in 1886 his portrait of the Misses Vickers was voted the worst picture of the year at the R.A., in a plebiscite organized by the *Pall Mall Gazette*. An example of his impressionism at this period is the unfinished picture of his sister Violet, entitled 'Lady Fishing' (page 22), which was painted at Fladbury in 1889. The placing of the white figure against the brilliant blue of the water, and the effect of sunlight on the grass, recall some of Monet's similiar studies of figures seen abruptly against sky or water, like his 'Girl with a Sunshade' of 1886 (in the Jeu de Paume). It is interesting to note that Sargent and Monet painted together at Giverny in 1888, which resulted in Sargent's 'Claude Monet Painting at the Edge of a Wood' (in the Tate Gallery).

In 1887 Sargent exhibited 'Carnation, Lily, Lily, Rose' (page 19) at the Royal Academy, a delightful contrast between the autumn twilight and the artificial light of the lanterns, the little girls in white dresses against the rich colours of the flowers. The treatment of light was very modern, but not obviously so, and the title and subject appealed to the sentimental Victorian public. It was bought by the Chantrey Bequest and proved enormously popular. Sargent's success was now assured, and a trip to the U.S.A. in the same year (only his second visit), where he was fêted by Boston and had more commissions for portraits than he could fulfil, re-emphasized this. America was to remain one of his most profitable sources of patronage.

In England Sargent came to full maturity as a painter; his

palette lightened (no more low-toned harmonies), his brushwork loosened and his style achieved a breath-taking simplicity and freedom. 'Lady Meyer and Her Two Children' (page 27) is an excellent example of this mature style and a remarkable tour-de-force. The fore-shortened perspective brings the figure of Lady Meyer steeply forward, and the design swirls upward via her arm and the back of the settee to the children. Silks, brocades, velvets, lace, even the book standing on end, are rendered with a sustained and passionate verve. For all its opulence and extravagant accessories, it is immensely vital, a portrait in the grand style, but alive with light and movement, a convincing portrayal of individuals in their social setting. No one else could match the effortless mastery of such a performance, and however much it may be criticised for its social implications, it painterly qualities are superb.

Sargent could, however, produce delightful and intimate studies, once away from the formality of the sitter's stand, which are couched in a very different language. Such is the painting called 'Mosquite Nets' (page 29) which shows his sister Emily and her friend Miss Wedgwood reading in the cool interior of a house in Corfu, their black dresses and the red cushions contrasting with the white wall behind. Painted rapidly, probably in a matter of hours, it has a revealing directness, the figures caught as in a snapshot, objects and the play of light on them rendered succinctly into paint. One can almost see Sargent stepping back to note the effect, then darting forward to place his brushstroke exactly where he intended, building up the composition in an entirely pragmatic way.

As time went on and Sargent tired of the demands of formal portraiture, he became more and more involved in such studies, and in landscapes and subject pictures. In the early 1900s he would spend much of his summer and autumn each year on sketching holidays in Italy, Spain or the Alps, with his family and friends. Painting in oil and water-colour he ceaselessly recorded his reactions to the play of light on architecture, rocks, water, figures, statues or whatever else caught his interest. The figure of a 'Nude Man Lying on a Bed' (page 29) has the same directness and informality as the 'Mosquito Nets', and is extremely modern in conception and composition. His oil landscapes, particularly his studies of his nieces in Alpine scenery, painted in thick impasto, light suffused into brilliant colour, have the same intensity as his best portraits.

Much of Sargent's time in later years (from 1890 till his death) was taken up with his murals for the Boston Library, and later for the Boston Museum—a vast undertaking but not a very successful one. They are couched in a largely dead classical language. Sargent was not an imaginative artist, but required the stimulus of the visible world.

Although portraiture began to bore him soon after the turn of the century (he referred to portraits as 'mugs' with a certain desperation), he could still rouse himself to his full powers when faced with a personality who challenged or fascinated him. The well-known portrait of his friend, Henry James (National Portrait Galley), with its dramatic and direct lighting, its sense of the very substance and mass of bone structure and flesh, and its absolute simplicity, is as characterful and masterly as anything he had painted.

Occasionally Sargent would do an oil sketch for a portrait, as in the case of Graham Robertson (page 21), where the figure is seen in terms of planes and tones. The finished portrait (Tate Gallery) is a superb image of an effete and elegant young man.

For the last fifteen years of his life Sargent refused to do any more portraits, with very occasional exceptions, which was a notable and unworldly act of protest. He was concerned with his sketches and his murals. His only concession to the hordes of wealthy and aristocratic people who clamoured to sit to him was the charcoal drawing. He turned them out at incredible speed and in great quantities, and here one does feel that he was almost forced to adopt a formula. It was rather a hit-or-miss affair, and many of the drawings express the boredom Sargent must have felt in doing them. One of the best is that of the Baroness de Meyer (page 28), a god-daughter of Edward VII, and a leader of Edwardian society in London and Paris. For here the image of the age does seem to be expressed through this imperious 'grande dame' who sums up the 'Belle Epoque', and is herself summed up in the slashing strokes of Sargent's charcoal.

LADY MEYER AND HER TWO CHILDREN, 1896
Coll. Sir Anthony Meyer, Bt.

Above: THE BARONESS DE MEYER, c. 1910. *City Art Gallery, Birmingham*

Opposite: NUDE MAN ON BED, 1917. *Coll. Conrad Ormond, Esq.*

[28]

Above: MOSQUITO NETS, 1908. *Coll. Conrad Ormond, Esq.*

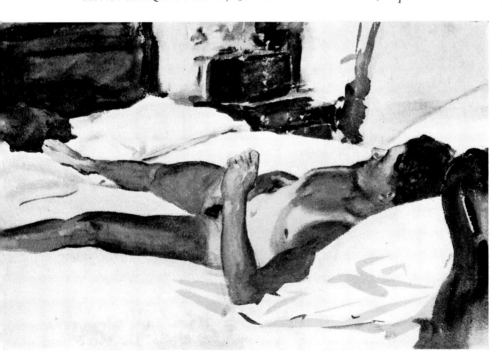

One of the serpentine bench-balustrades of the
Parque Güell, showing Gaudí's use of colour mosaic.

Antonio Gaudí

 SACHEVERELL SITWELL

PHOTOGRAPHS BY NORMAN PARKINSON

IN ORDER to understand, better still appreciate and enjoy, the buildings of Gaudí, it is helpful to have some knowledge of Barcelona, a city which is Catalan as much as and more than it is Spanish, and with a very personal life of its own of poverty and riches. Experience of this seething and tumultuous town can alter its values from hearing the cackling of the 'Capitoline' geese at their pool in the Cathedral cloister, 'kept there in reminder of the Roman greatness of Barcelona', to a nocturnal bull-fight where the clowns and the 'comedy' do not protect the bulls from dying of their wounds in the full glare of the floodlights; and from an evening's stroll down the Paralelo, with its theatres and music halls, its cinemas and cafés, to a late night in the low haunts of the Barrio de China where the stalls of the fun fair, the *baraques* of the strolling players and the murky dance-halls recalled till lately, perhaps still do even now, the clowns and harlequins of the 'blue period' of Picasso.

Add to all this the fantasies of Joan Miró, 'performing' to great success in the Tate Gallery in London of recent months, and the person of the supreme Catalan *fantaisiste*, Salvador Dalí, his elongated moustache, aerial transmitter or receiving set for ideas, whichever it is, his uncanny skill as a draughtsman, his often repeated intention of taking on and beating the camera at its own game, and all the rest of it, and we have a picture, or at least a sketch, of Barcelona.

> On the pale yellow sands
> There's a pair of clasped hands
> And an eyeball entangled in string,
> And a bicycle seat,
> And a plate of raw meat,
> And a thing that is *almost* a Thing.

So ran Lord Berners' poem describing Dalí's Surrealist paintings, his golden sands being those of the seaside resort of Rosas, the

Greek Rhoda, on the Costa Brava near the French frontier, and it could be said that the *fantaisie* of the Catalans extends from there all the way down to Valencia, where the Rococo Palacio de Dos Aguas, though of the eighteenth century, with its pale roses and greens, is in *Art Nouveau* taste and in its way worthy of Gaudí, and where the floats for the Fallas de San José in their easy luxuriance of pasteboard and *papier mâché* have on occasion been designed by Salvador Dalí.

In very midst of this golden shore, the *aprica littora* of the Roman poet Marcial, who came from not far inland at Bilbilis, the modern Calatayud, lies Reus, the town where Antonio Gaudí was born, well known to the present writer who has often stayed with friends who live near there. The year of Gaudí's birth was 1852, and for some thirty years after that little more is known of him. Because of this we have scant knowledge of the influences he felt or of the workings of his mind. But it would be wrong to think that these formative years were spent by him in a conscious effort to make himself original and unlike either contemporary or predecessor when opportunity came and he could begin building. There are certainly few if any traces of his developed style in the Bishop's Palace at Astorga, which was one of his first commissions, but, rather, in its Gothicism it is bleak and unpromising, like the dreary uplands round this town which is the capital of the wandering race of Maragatos. And yet it is almost contemporary with his first project for the Sagrada Familia, his acknowledged masterpiece, but in reality less interesting than other of his buildings in Barcelona.

But everybody who goes to Barcelona is taken past the Sagrada Familia, and therefore it is better to discuss it now. It is difficult to believe at first sight that this strange and utterly original building is as much as eighty years old; but in fact in its beginnings it dates from 1882. On catching sight of its four perforated and ugly steeples and caricature-Gothic finials let us keep our heads and remember we are in the Iberian Peninsula.

It was no less an authority than Grock who said, 'If Italy was the land of tenors, Spain was the land of clowns'—and Portugal, too, if the 'originals' or zanies of architecture are increased in number to include the Manoelino. In front of La Sagrada Familia we are on the Iberian mainland which has on its soil architectural fantasies and capriccios of the order of Juan Güas's Court of the Lions in the Infantado Palace at Guadalajara (unfortunately a casualty of the Spanish Civil War), or his no less extraordinary retablo-façades of two churches at Valladolid, one of them, that of San Gregorio, consisting of a huge shield with the royal arms upheld by supporters standing in the branches of a tree which in its turn shoots up from out of a fountain. The supporters are 'wild men' or satyrs, and the cresting or battlementing is of broken twigs. Juan Güas, a *fantaisiste* of the late fifteenth century, gave himself out to be a Frenchman or Burgundian, though names very near to his are to be noticed in the telephone book of Barcelona, and he may have been a Catalan pretending to be a foreigner. And other fantasies and *capriccios*, the interior of the Alhambra of Granada, the 'wanton excesses' of the Churriueresque such as the *Trasparente*, a piece of theatrical *trompe l'œil* behind the high altar of Toledo Cathedral, or the stalactitic parody of the Alhambra in the *Sacristía* of the Carthusian monastery at Granada, are matched at the other side of the peninsula by the interior of Belém outside Lisbon, which is Hindu in effect and inspiration, as Hindu as the *gopuram* gate tower and 'golden lily-tank' of Madura, and by the stone tie-sail bellying in the wind and framing a rose-window, the cords and ropes and sea-anemone motifs of the Convent of Christ at Tomar, the show place of the Manoelino, not forgetting the coral motif doorways in their flashing whiteness as though made of meerschaum or sea foam at the abbey church of Alcobaça.

I hope this list of Iberian architectural fantasies is not too long to take in, but once absorbed and digested it makes light of the peculiarities of La Sagrada Familia at Barcelona. It is less in the whole than in detail that we get the essential or true Gaudí: terminals striped like spike-flowers, like embryonic fingers, like mimosa sprays, or thistle heads. And, in no particular admiration of its unfinished interior, we leave La Sagrada Familia for a look at the other town buildings of Gaudi. It has been suggested before now that he was influenced by the mud buildings of Northern Africa and the Sudan, but if this may be true of La Sagrada Familia, which has certainly its counterpart in Saharan towns like Timimoun, we are now on different ground alto-gether. The exceedingly curious Casa Battló, which was built to simulate a breaking wave, and has a roof with a cresting of green tiles to represent the foam and spray, is, I note, almost exactly contemporary (1905–7) with Debussy's *La Mer* (1903–5), and I have suggested elsewhere that Gaudí, like Debussy, admired Hokusai's woodcut of the Great Wave.

The Casa Milá, an apartment house nearly opposite, in the Paseo de Gracia, has been said to be in the shape of the holy mountain of Montserrat, outside Barcelona, with waving balconies to suggest its striations and dolomitic formations, an inference which I think is a little too far-fetched. But it is indeed curious enough to need no further excuse or apology. We reproduce its chimney-cowls, to which Gaudí has given necks, Tuareg-like head-wrappings, helmet tops, and all but eyes. One or two of these chimney-cowls are carried even further until they resemble the mysterious giant statue-heads on Easter Island. Downstairs in the Casa Milá, where Gaudí in advance of his day made provision for lifts and not for staircases, the entrance hall is monolithic but made of cement and not stone, and taking every advantage from the propensity or even preference of cement to be worked and treated in this manner. Upstairs, looking along the façade, the windows are like portholes with their lids raised, and the balconies seem to be formed of bracken, dead leaves, and the sort of litter left about after a picnic.

Or so it seems, for on another day it might, like music, seem to mean or portray something quite different. Not so, however, the metal rail of another house in Barcelona, the Casa Vicens, in Calle Carolinas, which is unmistakably formed of large palm-fronds worked into circles and making a perfectly sensible and natural iron railing. But the utmost fantasies of Gaudí were practised for the Güell family; and no one who remembers, as I do, Don Eusebio Güell, who lived as a child in their town house, now in midst of the hectic night life of the Barrio de China, and at the Parque Güell, could wonder or be surprised at his fantastic person and the funambulist air of everything about him. He was the true child of the strange buildings that Gaudí thought up for his family. I cannot admit to an admiration

Gaudí made great use of colour mosaic formed of broken tiles and red cups and saucers. In the background of this photograph can be seen the spires of the Familia Sagrada.

An instance of Gaudí at work in metal: a conglomerate of palm-frond, serpent or sea-snake, and bat's wing.

A balcony at the Casa Milá. The motifs are difficult to identify, but suggest dead leaves and litter.

Chimney cowls at the Casa Milá in Barcelona.
Gaudí has given them human, if spectral, interest.
Strange apparitions in masks and visors, they
loom like cement ghosts above the noisy street.

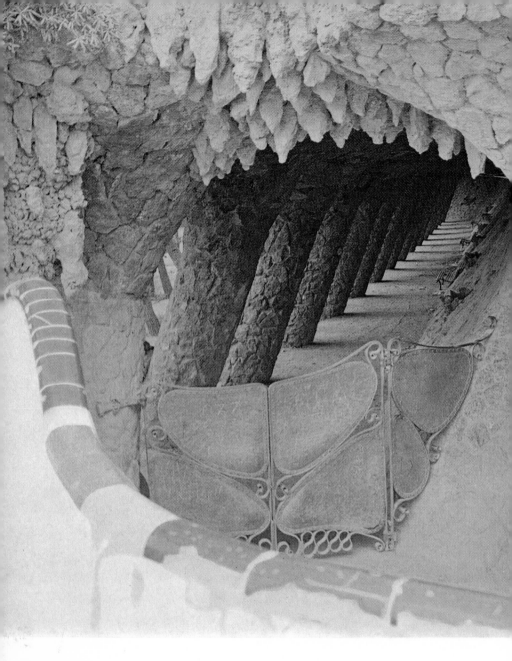

The entrance to one of the grotto corridors of the Parque Güell, giving on to reeling columns. Fun-fair or Musée Guérin effects.

for the lodges of the Parque Güell. They are Disney-like and reminiscent of *Snow White and the Seven Dwarfs*. But it is at the Parque Güell that Gaudí's colour play can be seen at its most inventive, and where the invitation of his patrons was to be light-hearted and not serious. In this gay setting he made full use of a decorative art which is essentially Iberian, whether we think of it as Moorish tilework as seen in the patios of Seville and along the coast of the Levante or in the *azulejos* of Portugal. But Gaudí gave a new turn to the art, and in his hands the mosaics of broken bits of coloured pottery and cement become typical of the *Art Nouveau* while employing a technique more like that used in the panto-mime temples of Bangkok. This is particularly the case with his winding, serpentine balustrades, snake-like of convolution and gayer of intent than the markings of rattle-snake or cobra.

That the Parque Güell is some form of permanent fun-fair or entertainment is not to be denied, and one may be reminded by it of the so called *guingette* that the Prince Regent wished to build in the middle of Regent's Park, *guingette* meaning a pleasure resort and implying 'that the Prince's intentions were of a holiday nature'. The Parque Güell, likewise, is built just outside the town, and cannot have been intended for solitary contem-plation or solemn reverie. Its other curious features include tree-caryalids in stone, with baskets of flowers on their heads, and a terrace with huge pebble baskets carrying palms that have their roots simulated in pebble work at eye-level as you walk past. There are, as well, *columnas hirsutas* which seem to have begun by imitating the trunks of palm trees and then decided to grow hairy, but in fact stony, excrescences in all directions, and long galleries with columns leaning inwards, of reeling, drunken effect. All this from a person of solitary, recluse char-acter and deep, almost fanatic religious conviction; a genius of his kind beyond question and a very Spanish genius at that.

Was Gaudí, like Henry van de Velde, and most of the creators of *Art Nouveau*, including of course Englishmen like Voysey and Mackintosh, a fervent reader of Ruskin and disciple of William Morris? I must admit to finding no trace whatever of Ruskin in the buildings of Gaudí. In this as in everything else he seems to have been the great 'original' of his age.

c*

Poems of the 'Nineties

THE WELL-KNOWN poets of the time are not here—Yeats, Hardy, Kipling, A. E. Housman (though he is *fin-de-siècle*), nor even Lionel Johnson. Only the glorious Ernest Dowson is admitted who, more than all, stirred the languid lilies of this particular pool. Of him, there is one of the less anthologised poems. Mostly it is poetry of despair and escape. The end of all things seemed at hand and the mood is not confined to the 'nineties. It can be found in the exotic poems of Theo Marzials and Gordon Hake and Swinburne in the 'seventies and it lingered on in the poems of Edmund John which were published in 1913, and then the real end of all things happened with the First World War. It was goodbye to absinthe, stramony, Liberty silks, tulip shapes and the Café Royal.

These poems are arranged not chronologically but according to moods characteristic of late-Victorian and Edwardian poesie. We might have made a trip wi' the wee fairy folk o'er the heather wi' 'Fiona Macleod' or burnt a tall candle with Maire, wife of Shemus Rua, before a shrine in olden Ireland with the early Yeats or read in branching Ogham the translations of Douglas Hyde, but it seemed to me that there was so much to include beside the Celtic mood that I would confine us to the English strand, with longings for the Paris of Verlaine, the Italy of Corvo, the Greece of Narcissus, and the swirling incense of London, Brighton and South Coast religion.

Mark André Raffalovich, who lived in Edinburgh with his friend, Father John Gray, until well within living memory, wrote, in a poem 'To Ralph Nevil':

> But now I never, never murmur
> The foolish things so light to tell:
> Though words should struggle, I am firmer
> And keep them prisoned well.

This is just what the other poets in this brief selection did *not* do. These uninhibited *fin-de-siècle* writers did not mind what they said. But what they said, they expressed clearly, with a great sense of the sound of words and often a wealth of innuendo.

I could have wished that this preface had been one of Hubert Crackanthorpe's prose poems.

 LONDON

LONDON had been rediscovered by Whistler. Fog is beautiful. Hansoms, in Richard le Gallienne's phrase, are like 'dragonflies with jewelled eyes'. Bought women lie in gaslit rooms. Sin, drugs and impending suicide stalk the streets.

ATHWART the sky a lowly sigh
    From west to east the sweet wind carried;
    The sun stood still on Primrose Hill;
His light in all the city tarried:
The clouds on viewless columns bloomed
Like smouldering lilies unconsumed.

Oh sweetheart, see! how shadowy,
    Of some occult magician's wearing,
Or swung in space of heaven's grace
    Dissolving, dimly reappearing,
Afloat upon ethereal tides
St. Paul's above the city rides.

A rumour broke through the thin smoke
    Enwreathing abbey, tower, and palace
The parks, the squares, the thoroughfares,
    The million-peopled lanes and alleys,
An ever-muttering prisoned storm
The heart of London beating warm.

JOHN DAVIDSON: *Ballads and Songs*, 1894

A NORTHERN SUBURB

Nature selects the longest way,
  And winds about in tortuous grooves;
  A thousand years the oaks decay;
The wrinkled glacier hardly moves.

But here the whetted fangs of change
  Daily devour the old demesne—
The busy farm, the quiet grange,
  The wayside inn, the village green.

In gaudy yellow brick and red,
  With rooting pipes, like creepers rank,
The shoddy terraces o'erspread
  Meadow, and garth, and daisied bank.

With shelves for rooms the houses crowd,
  Like draughty cupboards in a row—
Ice-chests when wintry winds are loud,
  Ovens when summer breezes blow.

Roused by the fee'd policeman's knock
  And sad that day should come again,
Under the stars the workmen flock
  In haste to reach the workmen's train.

For here dwell those who must fulfil
  Dull tasks in uncongenial spheres,
Who toil through dread of coming ill,
  And not with hope of happier years—

The lowly folk who scarcely dare
  Conceive themselves perhaps misplaced,
Whose prize for unremitting care
  Is only not to be disgraced.

JOHN DAVIDSON: *New Ballads*, 1897

SUNDAY AFTERNOON

IT WAS a little street, shabbily symmetrical—a double row of insignificant, dingy-brick houses. Muffled in the dusk of the fading winter afternoon, it seemed sunk in squalid, listless slumber. In the distance a church-bell was tolling its joyless mechanical Sunday tale.

A man stood in the roadway, droning the words of a hymn-tune. He was old and decayed and sluttish: he wore an ancient, baggy frock-coat, and through the cracks in his boots you could see the red flesh of his feet. His gait was starved and timid: the touch of the air was very bitter. And when he had finished his singing, he remained gazing up at the rows of lifeless windows, with a look of dull expectancy in his bloodshot, watery eyes.

HUBERT CRACKANTHORPE: *Vignettes*, 1896

A LONDON PLANE-TREE

GREEN is the plane-tree in the square,
   The other trees are brown;
They droop and pine for country air;
   The plane-tree loves the town.

Here from my garret-pane, I mark
   The plane-tree bud and blow,
Shed her recuperative bark,
   And spread her shade below.

Among her branches, in and out,
   The city breezes play;
The dun fog wraps her round about;
   Above, the smoke curls grey.

Others the country take for choice,
   And hold the town in scorn;
But she has listened to the voice
   On city breezes borne.

AMY LEVY: *A London Plane-Tree*, 1889

STRAW IN THE STREET

STRAW in the street where I pass today
Dulls the sound of the wheels and feet.
'Tis for a failing life they lay
    Straw in the street.

Here, where the pulses of London beat,
Someone strives with the Presence grey;
Ah, is it victory or defeat?

The hurrying people go their way,
Pause and jostle and pass and greet;
For life, for death, are they treading, say,
    Straw in the street?

AMY LEVY: *A London Plane-Tree*, 1889

IN BOHEMIA

DRAWN blinds and flaring gas within,
    And wine, and women, and cigars;
    Without, the city's heedless din;
Above, the white unheeding stars.

And we, alike from each remote,
    The world that works, the heaven that waits,
Con our brief pleasures o'er by rote,
    The favourite pastime of the Fates.

We smoke, to fancy that we dream,
    And drink, a moment's joy to prove,
And fain would love, and only seem
    To love because we cannot love.

Draw back the blinds, put out the light!
    'Tis morning, let the daylight come.
God, how the women's cheeks are white,
    And how the sunlight strikes us dumb!

ARTHUR SYMONS: *Silhouettes*, 1892

WOMEN

SHE-WHO-MUST-BE-OBEYED is a creature of inexplicable moods, whom we menfolk reverence as a precious plaything. Sometimes if She gets out of hand, and becomes a political hostess, we do not like Her.

SHE IS NOT OLD, she is not young
The Woman with the Serpent's Tongue,
The haggard cheek, the hungering eye,
The poisoned words that wildly fly,
The famished face, the fevered hand,—
Who slights the worthiest in the land,
Sneers at the just, contemns the brave,
And blackens goodness in its grave.

In truthful numbers be she sung
The Woman with the Serpent's Tongue;
Concerning whom, Fame hints at things
Told but in shrugs and whisperings:
Ambitious from her natal hour,
And scheming all her life for power;
With little left of seemly pride;
With venomed fangs she cannot hide;
Who half makes love to you today,
Tomorrow gives her guest away.
Burnt up within by that strange soul
She cannot slake, or yet control:
Malignant-lipped, unkind, unsweet;
Past all example indiscreet;
Hectic, and always overstrung,—
The Woman with the Serpent's Tongue.

To think that such as she can mar
Names that among the noblest are!
That hands like hers can touch the springs
That move who knows what men and things?
That on *her* will *their* fates have hung!—
The Woman with the Serpent's Tongue.

SIR WILLIAM WATSON: *New Poems,* 1909

IN THE SEASON

HER INSOLENT carriage shines down Rotten Row,
   Her beauty shaded from the sun of June
   Outblazes even the dazzling afternoon;
Her heart is hard and hot with triumph; though
Her eyelids droop too languid to bestow
   A glance upon the crowd that drives or stands,
   She feels the reins of conquest in her hands,
Exulting in the senses' overthrow.

The champing horses bear her down the mile,
And as all eyes go after her a smile
   Dawns and is gone upon the clear-cut face;
She leans back on the cushions to recall
The night's long list of dinner, theatre, ball,
   In languors of premeditated grace.

THEODORE WRATISLAW: *Caprices*, 1893

A SONG

STEAL from the meadows, rob the tall green hills,
   Ravish my orchard's blossoms, let me bind
   A crown of orchard flowers and daffodils,
Because my love is fair and white and kind.

Today the thrush has trilled her daintiest phrases,
   Flowers with their incense have made drunk the air,
God has bent down to gild the hearts of daisies,
   Because my love is kind and white and fair.

Today the sun has kissed the rose-tree's daughter,
   And sad Narcissus, Spring's pale acolyte,
Hangs down his head and smiles into the water,
   Because my love is kind and fair and white.

LORD ALFRED DOUGLAS: *The City of the Soul*, 1899

[46]

LOVE can be given to girl or boy. Passion is sensuous, and twines around one's heart like waterlily stems in the river of life. In dark streets there are strange sins connected, perhaps, with 'the love that dare not speak its name'.

HEART'S DEMESNE
To Paul Verlaine

LISTEN, bright lady, thy deep Pansie eyes
Made never answer when my eyes did pray,
Than with those quaintest looks of blank surprise.

But my lovelonging has devised a way
To mock thy living image, from thy hair
To thy rose toes; and keep thee by alway.

My garden's face is oh! so maidly fair,
With limbs all tapering and with hues all fresh;
Thine are the beauties all that flourish there.

Amaranth, fadeless, tells me of thy flesh.
Briarrose knows thy cheek, the Pink thy pout.
Bunched kisses dangle from the Woodbine mesh.

I love to loll, when Daisy stars peep out,
And hear the music of my garden dell,
Hollyhock's laughter and the Sunflower's shout.

And many whisper things I dare not tell.

JOHN GRAY: *Silverpoints*, 1893

THE DEAD POET

I DREAMED of him last night, I saw his face
All radiant and unshadowed of distress,
And as of old, in music measureless,
I heard his golden voice and marked him trace
Under the common thing the hidden grace,
And conjure wonder out of emptiness,
Till mean things put on beauty like a dress
And all the world was an enchanted place.

And then methought outside a fast locked gate
I mourned the loss of unrecorded words,
Forgotten tales and mysteries half said,
Wonders that might have been articulate,
And voiceless thoughts like murdered singing birds.
And so I woke and knew that he was dead.

LORD ALFRED DOUGLAS: Sonnets, 1909

A SYMPHONY of blues and brown—
We were together in the town:
A grimy tavern with blurred walls,
Where dingy lamplight floats and falls
On working men and women, clad
In sober watchet, umber sad.
Two viols and one 'cello scream
Waltz music through the smoke and steam:
You rise, you clasp a comrade, who
Is clothed in triple blues like you:
Sunk in some dream voluptuously
Circle those azures richly blent,
Swim through the dusk, the melody;
Languidly breathing, you and he,
Uplifting the environment;
Ivory face and swart face laid
Cheek unto cheek, like man, like maid.

JOHN ADDINGTON SYMONDS: In the Key of Blue, 1893

PASSIONAL

WHAT does it matter though you shall forget?
Leave it: I hold your warm slim body yet,
Heart against mine, so that your fragrant breath
Falls on my lips, chanting a marvellous song
Most strange and beautiful, though over-long
For one whose heart shall throb itself to death.

I know your lips shall kindle other flames,
Your dawn-lit voice shall whisper distant names:
You, with the kissed hands of Love's acolyte,
The perfume of the night in your wild hair,
Like sad strange incense, like a pagan prayer . . .
I care not, since I hold you here tonight.

Harder, press harder with your scarlet mouth,
That your kiss sear me with the flaming South,
That your frail unstained youth like pain of June
Crush my strong soul your soul's enchantment grips . . .
Cling to my mouth with your young curved Greek lips,
Cling closer till the blood come and life swoon . . .

God, hold the pallid dawn that thou wouldst send
With slow grey fingers that shall spell the end,
When I must leave my soul and you—ah, sweet!
Let me weep here a moment, let me kneel,
And give you tears for Love's, for Sorrow's seal,
And bow my head, and kiss your sad young feet.

Yes, close your eyes, lie still . . . as death . . .
My lips hold yet the memory of your breath . . .
The feverish yellow moon is on the wane;
Closer it comes, silent, and mad, and vast,
With blackness round and dead shapes stealing past,
And splashed with one wild blood-red line of pain.

EDMUND JOHN: *The Flute of Sardonyx,* 1913

[49]

SLENDER COLUMNS in the style known as 'late Gothic freely treated' rise to vaulted roofs. Windows of bluish green by Kempe shine down on veined marble, and the gold lamps gleam in the Sanctuary beyond the many-coloured rood screen. Incense floats with love and passion in worship, canticle and prayer.

EXTREME UNCTION

UPON the eyes, the lips, the feet,
   On all the passages of sense,
   The atoning oil is spread with sweet
Renewal of lost innocence.

The feet, that lately ran so fast
   To meet desire, are soothly sealed;
The eyes, that were so often cast
   On vanity, are touched and healed.

From troublous sights and sounds set free;
   In such a twilight hour of breath,
Shall one retrace his life, or see,
   Through shadows, the true face of death?

Vials of mercy! Sacring oils!
   I know not where nor when I come,
Nor through what wanderings and toils,
   To crave of you Viaticum.

Yet, when the walls of flesh grow weak,
   In such an hour, it well may be,
Through mist and darkness, light will break,
   And each anointed sense will see.

ERNEST DOWSON: *Verses,* 1896

THE ACOLYTE

SOLEMN the stained light lies
    Like Love upon the cool calm stones
    That seal a slow, forgotten music deep—
The dim dirge of the dreamless dead in sleep
Chanting in mediaeval tones.

Solemn the obscure height,
The purple gloom of the groined roof:
And the fine tracery of arch and shrine
Is as life's thin spun threads that twist and twine,
Woven all wanly in the woof.

Solemn the avenue
Of silent stone and pillared thought,
Leading to where the mystic seven lamps gleam
Before the ancient altar of a dream
Of succour that the dead once sought.

Solemn the crucifix
That rises where the faint flowers float,
Calm symbol of the wounded world's wild pain,
For all whose wan white lips have smiled in vain
While salt tears rattled in their throat.

Through the solemnity,
Warm through the solemn holiness,
The sensuous song of incense sighing low
Is lingering subtly from a noon ago,
Like love at death, like pride in lowliness.

I saw thy shining eyes
Upraised and marvellously bright,
Lit with the faint fire of a dream's fleet breath,
And thy soul flaming strangely into death,
And thy cheeks pale, and thy red lips alight.

Yea, but thy wide eyes burned
Like stars above a pagan shrine;
And in them shone a gleam of pagan things,
And mystic rite, and shadow of Love's wings,
Of Dionysus and spilled wine.

And like to Lesbian wine,
And the fleet gods' white limbs, and flame,
Were crimson cassock and fair lace on thee:
And on thy brow were written wondrously
The letters of a Greek god's name.

About the crucifix,
Borne slow for all ye slow to follow,
Amyclaean scents of Hyacinthus hung,
And from the dead eyes of the Christ was flung,
Swiftly, the live glance of Apollo.

From swaying thurible,
From bronzéd censers slowly swung,
Rose holy vapours mingled with desire;
And the red charcoal glowed like altar-fire
Of some white temple when the gods were young.

Then through the monkish hymn
A strange note and a piercing sweetness ran;
And a young priest, who saw thee, clutched his beads,
And grew all pale as from the organ reeds
Pealed once the poignant pipes of Pan.

Who art thou, Acolyte?
Whose breath makes sweet the God of Sighs?
What lips have kissed thy lithe lips into flame?
Nay, but I know not, would not know thy name—
For I am stricken by thine eyes. . . .

EDMUND JOHN: *The Flute of Sardonyx,* 1913

[52]

CHILDHOOD is recalled as a Golden Age of roguish innocence. The Arcadian theme is also expressed in a love for Sussex dairymaids and drinking out of pocket-mugs nigh Poynings, hidden by the Downs from the false stucco of Brighton.

PEACOCKS: A MOOD

IN GORGEOUS plumage, azure, gold and green,
    They trample the pale flowers, and their shrill cry
    Troubles the garden's bright tranquillity!
Proud birds of Beauty, splendid and serene,
Spreading their brilliant fans, screen after screen
    Of burnished sapphire, gemmed with mimic suns—
    Strange magic eyes that, so the legend runs,
Will bring misfortune to this fair demesne. . . .

And my gay youth, that, vain and debonair,
    Sits in the sunshine—tired at last of play
    (A child, that finds the morning all too long),
Tempts with its beauty that disastrous day
When in the gathering darkness of despair
    Death shall strike dumb the laughing mouth of song.

OLIVE CUSTANCE (*Lady Alfred Douglas*): *The Inn of Dreams*, 1911

PADDY MALOY

O PADDY MALOY is a broth of a boy,
    As pretty as pretty can be;
    He tosses his curls in disdain at the girls,
For not one is so pretty as he.

Though he's seven years old, he's a bachelor bold,
    As for marrying, simply he *won't*;
His papa's in despair, for you see he's the heir,
    And the line will run out if he don't.

If a lady but touch him, his anger is such
That he flushes as red as a rose;
But if he is kissed, in a moment his fist
Goes simply straight bang at her nose!

What to do with a boy like young Paddy Maloy
Is a problem to puzzle a sage;
I'm thinking, *ochone*! we must leave him alone,
For it's too late to change at his age.

THE REV. E. E. BRADFORD: *Sonnets, Songs and Ballads*, 1908

RUM AND MILK

Now SOME may drink to ladies fine,
  With painted cheeks and gowns of silk;
  But we will drink to dairymaids,
In pocket-mugs of rum and milk!
  O, 'tis up in the morning early,
    When the dew is on the grass,
  And St. John's bell rings for matins,
    And St. Mary's rings for mass!

The merry skylarks soar and sing,
  And seem to Heaven very near—
Who knows what blessed inns they see,
  What holy drinking songs they hear?
    O, 'tis etc. etc.

The mushrooms may be priceless pearls
  A queen has lost beside the stream,
But rum is melted rubies when
  It turns the milk to golden cream.
    O, 'tis etc. etc.

CHARLES WILLIAM DALMON: *Song Favours*, 1895

ROBERT BEVAN

1865–1925

A Sale at Tattersall's, 1911. Coll. Lt.-Col. J. K. McConnel

A CENTENARY TRIBUTE BY J. WOOD PALMER

Above: FROM THE ARTIST'S WINDOW, 1916. *Leicester Art Gallery*

Below: ADELAIDE ROAD IN SUNLIGHT, 1909–10. *Coll. R. A. Bevan, Esq.*

In the society that existed in England during the earlier part of this century an interest in the visual arts was not an element that counted. The Edwardians were too surfeited with wealth to exercise any enterprising taste; and artists with ideas that did not conform to academic standards were largely ignored. Impressionism, even, was still suspect, and anything beyond that an aberration not to be seriously considered. From this stony ground, with the usual illogicality, there arose a flowering of talent which is now belatedly recognised as one of the most influential schools of painting Britain has ever known.

An artist may be important without being necessarily an inspiration to succeeding generations, and while several individualists in England at the turn of the century built up for themselves a reputation that has stood the test of time, it was left to no more than three—Harold Gilman, Spencer Gore and Robert Bevan—to canalize the powerful post-Impressionist movement which in France was expressed most clearly in the work of Van Gogh, Cézanne and Gauguin.

Gore and Bevan, unlike most artists of the time in that they were accustomed to visiting the continent, had in a way a flying start of the others, and when Roger Fry introduced into London in 1910 the post-Impressionist artists from France the revelation was not such a shock to these two artists as to their less travelled contempories. Bevan, alone among them, had worked in the vicinity of one of the Masters, having spent the best part of two years, in 1893 and 1894, at Pont Aven at the same time as Gauguin. It is at this period in his career that the foundations were laid of his very personal style, a style in no sense a pastiche of Gauguin, but so clearly based on him that it can be seen now as a prophecy in his time of the death of Impressionism in England.

In the artist's earlier work the Gauguin influence was not immediately apparent. Possibly such a powerful leaven had to take time to work itself to the top. The drawings in Brittany, such as 'Shadows on the Road' (page 59), show much more an awareness of Van Gogh, and of this kind 'The Sabot Makers', exhibited in London in 1956, is a notable example. In the sketchbooks of that time also are many drawings of Port Aven scenes and peasants which are simplified in planes and mass in no way

D

at all. Later, when he was painting in Poland, the work varies from a frank Impressionism with echoes of Pissarro to an extraordinary group of studies culminating in one painting, 'The Courtyard, Poland', which is astonishing for any English artist to have produced at that time. A strange hybrid, with the expressionist swirl of Munch and the uninhibited palette of Gauguin, it caused such a stir when exhibited in London and gave the critics so golden an opportunity to rend that Bevan was discouraged from pursuing a path that might have led him to a moderately extreme *fauvisme*. Instead he turned back to Impressionism in *divisioniste* technique though still employing colour of a wider range than nature could conveniently offer, as can be seen in 'Ploughing on the Downs', 1910 (Aberdeen Art Gallery). This method continued and is evident in the earlier Cab Yards and Horse Sales, the supreme example of which is 'Cab Yard at Night', 1910 (Brighton Art Gallery), but had already begun to disappear by 1911, in 'A Sale at Tattersalls', and to be replaced by a greater emphasis on construction and, in the Horse Sale

THREE HORSES, SUSSEX, 1905. *Coll. R. A. Bevan, Esq.*

SHADOWS ON THE ROAD, BRITTANY, c. 1894. *Coll. J. Wood Palmer, Esq.*

paintings, interesting experiments of opposed diagonals in some compositions. By 1913 the Gauguin influence had come into its own and remained with him for the rest of his painting career.

Before the First World War the lot of *avant-garde* artists in England was not a happy one. Concentration on painting was only the beginning of their difficulties; they had as well to exercise every ingenuity to find somewhere to exhibit their work, let alone sell it. The result was a tendency among artists to band together and pool their efforts to force the attention of cautious dealers and an indifferent public. Robert Bevan took his full share in organising artists with this end in view. Looked upon with chill by the New English Art Club which, originally a body in revolt against the Royal Academy, had itself developed hardening of the artistic arteries, he was one of the prime movers in splitting away from it to form the Camden Town Group in 1911, and when this died an untimely death he became one of the original members of the London Group. The Cumberland Market Group, which met and painted in rooms he had taken overlooking the market, was, in 1915, particularly his creation, and the paintings he produced of the market and market carts, and horses at rest in their nosebags, are, in their high key, a special if limited part of his *œuvre*.

At this date also appeared a number of London street scenes which, in their planned sobriety, reflected more truthfully than has the work of any other artist of that time the cult of moderation inherited by the English bourgeoisie from classical Greece and turned by them into the dread Anglo-Saxon reserve. In this milieu cautiously sustained by tea and Consols, Sickert explored the lesser bedrooms, Ginner examined in wearing detail the back gardens and the kitchen windows, Spencer Gore illumined with lilac the languidly perspiring tennis-players in the Crescent gardens (to which every householder jealously guarded a key), but only Bevan knew the true value of façade, though he was too much a gentleman to hint at anything that lay behind, since the English cannot stomach disclosure.

Of these street scenes the early 'Adelaide Road in Sunlight' bears not the least resemblance to the later version in Boston. It is a most tender and brilliant outburst of colour in the Impressionist manner whereas the painting of 1920 is extreme in its hard planning and elimination of anything as spurious as charm. *Tour de force* in pursuit of a formula it may be, but when it is remembered how warming and acceptable is the earlier essay it is a relief to find that this particular flight on the artist's part was his limit, and at the end of the long vista of Adelaide Road Wyndham Lewis and his entourage beckoned in vain.

It is perhaps odd to write about this artist without concentrating on the most widely known aspect of his work, the paintings of horses, cab yards, horse sales and so on. Certainly these paintings show him at his best, and are so unique a contribution to English art that posterity will mention him with Stubbs and Marshall and Ferneley. But posterity is a long way off. What is being realised now is that Robert Bevan was an innovator in one of the most fertile periods in English art history, the decade before the First World War, and that his work will last long after much of the junk we suffer today has met its fifth of November.

Aubrey
Beardsley

A REAPPRAISAL BY W. G. GOOD

AUBREY BEARDSLEY gave his name to a period in English
art and letters, but in the decades after his death he did not
command widespread attention. In recent years, however,
the 'Beardsley period' has been, in common with *Art Nouveau*, the
subject of renewed interest. The great changes which have come
about since the turn of the century result in the period being
far more distant from us in spirit than a normal life span, and
the time has come when it can be seen with fresh eyes.

Beardsley was born at Brighton in August, 1872, and died in
March, 1898. For one with so short a working life the quantity of
his output was remarkable, and the speed and range of his
development astonishing. Signs of the tuberculosis which
killed him were evident from childhood, and, as may be seen

from his letters, behind the alternate hopes and despairs occasioned by his rallies and relapses there was the grim presage, most courageously sustained, that his life would be short. He worked with feverish energy, passing from childish drawings to the highest technical mastery in a decade. It is profitless to speculate concerning the advances he might have made had he lived longer, but it is probable that he had already given of the most which was in him; that the world lost many a lovely drawing is certain, but it is unlikely that the quality of the best which we have could have been much exceeded.

Beardsley was intelligent, but his mind was not of the commanding order of genius whose work induces a sense of awe by its intellectual force. Content, to the extent that his malady and the modest rewards of his work allowed, to enjoy the good things of life, he had no message for the world, no philosophy to propound. Elements of caricature, of eroticism, and of pure lyrical loveliness are seen in his work, but when he sat down to draw his dominant intention was no more than to 'make a picture'. Thus it is that although many of his designs are striking in content, their main appeal lies in his skill in employment of pen and ink and particularly in the immense clarity, strength and sureness of his line. Beardsley in modern issues of his work has often been ill served, the printing blocks having been made from reproductions, with consequent loss of definition. In preparing the illustrations for the present article pains have been taken to work wherever possible from the drawings themselves, and the artist's limpid brilliance is seen at only one stage removed.

Commissioned to illustrate an edition of *Le Morte Darthur* which was issued in parts, the first in June, 1893, Beardsley made approximately 350 chapter headings, one of which appears at the head of this article, and other designs. No great evidence of his future mastery appears, but the work imposed a discipline and practice which brought their reward. Before this task was complete he was engaged in illustrating Wilde's *Salome*, from which 'The Stomach Dance' is here reproduced. In this is seen his skill in the handling of black and white masses and in the portrayal of the human figure, the forward thrust of the dancer's body being most vividly conveyed.

IT IS SAID that the publisher, John Lane, aware of the impish
delight which Beardsley took in introducing improper
detail into his drawings, scrutinised the Salome set with
special care. Two drawings, indeed, were bowdlerised for publication, but Lane's perception evidently failed him when he
examined the demoniac musician in the present design.

THE SALOME drawings, sometimes irrelevant (Salome performed the dance of the seven veils), impudent (two designs contain caricatures of Wilde) and erotic, show in their swirling, sinuous lines the influence of the Japanese colour print and of *Art Nouveau*. They were successful and have always deservedly attracted more attention than the play. The book was published in February, 1894, at about which time Lane planned *The Yellow Book*, 'An Illustrated Quarterly', appointing Beardsley as art editor. Above appears his strong cover design for Volume I, issued in April. The simple, yet most effective, treatment of the face of the woman shows the vein of caricature so often present in his work.

Beardsley's four other designs for the first number were made conspicuous by their bold use of black and white masses and suggestive insouciance of style. The issue was a popular success and London 'turned yellow overnight'. Censorious voices, of course, were heard: *The Times*, referring particularly to the cover design, spoke of 'repulsiveness and insolence . . . a combination of English rowdyism with French lubricity'. But Beardsley's brief hour of general acclaim had come.

B EARDSLEY contributed to the next three numbers of *The
Yellow Book*, and the 'Wagnerites', from Volume 3, is shown
here. Alive with satirical observation, it is technically a
magnificent achievement. By a mere outline and with no
shading, Beardsley was able to render moulding, and even
texture, as in the smooth, rounded firmness revealed by the
décolletage of the women. His power to suggest form, notwith-
standing an unbroken background of black, may be seen in the
figures in the foreground; it has been said that he could 'draw
black on black'.

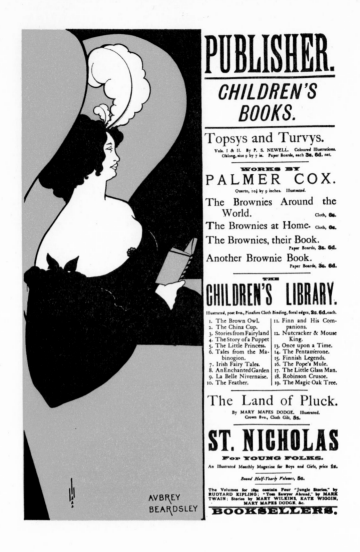

DURING the 'nineties great interest was taken in the poster as an art form, and attention was paid to it by artists of merit. The posters of Toulouse-Lautrec were seen by Beardsley, and the walls of Paris were brightened also by the studied friviolities of Chéret, Steinlen and Willette. The work in England of the Beggarstaff Brothers is well known. Beardsley designed several posters and wrote an article, *The Art of the Hoarding:* 'Beauty has laid siege to the city, and telegraph wires shall no longer be the sole joy of our aesthetic perceptions.'

THE Children's Books poster for T. Fisher Unwin is notable
for its breadth and simplicity of design, an essential to
success which is the outcome of the careful calculation
which may be seen in the conformity of the curves of the breast,
the feather and the wing of the chair. The subject possibly had
less appeal to youthful readers than to their fathers. In the design
for *The Spinster's Scrip* the artist's happy facility in making use
of costume is evident; other examples of this skill appear in the
following pages.

AB.

IN 1896 appeared an edition of Pope's *The Rape of the Lock* 'embroidered' by Beardsley. His designs are triumphal, both in reflecting the mood of the poem and in artistic skill. Particularly noteworthy are the drawing of the folds of the sleeve and the foreshortening of the figure in 'The New Star', above, and the rendering of material surfaces in 'The Battle of the Beaux and the Belles'. His famous 'dotted line' demanded the greatest control of hand and pen.

THE SCANDAL of the Wilde trials in the spring of 1895 induced Lane, unjustly, for the artist's appetites were entirely normal, to dismiss Beardsley, and thereafter his work was published by Leonard Smithers. In January, 1896, *The Savoy* was launched. Two numbers in pink boards were followed by six in blue paper, all with cover designs by the artist, that for No. 1 appearing here. *The Yellow Book* in the foreground, for which the manikin is showing his contempt, was removed from the published design.

The idyllic scene above was used for the prospectus for Volume V of *The Yellow Book*, although in the volume itself all Beardsley's contributions were suppressed. The design was later adapted for the covers of two of Smithers' Catalogues of Rare Books.

The Savoy contained some of Beardsley's best work, and two examples appear overleaf. 'The Abbé' illustrated his own 'Romantic Novel', *Venus and Tannhäuser*, of which a heavily expurgated version was printed in the magazine as *Under the Hill*. The artist's love of music was reflected in several fine designs, such as the Third Tableau of *Das Rheingold*.

THE flowing freedom of design and the firm, supple outline of the figure make 'Apollo pursuing Daphne' particularly successful. The drawing is unfinished and in the original the left foot is pencilled in. It was Beardsley's method to sketch in a design, building it up and changing it as he worked. When its final form was arrived at, he inked over the pencil, disregarding all superfluous lines.

The lovely 'Ave atque Vale' appeared in *The Savoy*, illustrating Beardsley's translation from Catullus. This has genuine poetic feeling, and the same painstaking elaboration was lavished on the poem as on the drawings.

BY WAYS remote and distant waters sped,
Brother, to thy sad grave-side am I come,
That I may give the last gifts to the dead,
And vainly parley with thine ashes dumb:
Since she who now bestows and now denies
Hath ta'en thee, hapless brother, from mine eyes.

But lo! these gifts, the heirlooms of past years,
Are made sad things to grace thy coffin shell,
Take them, all drenchèd with a brother's tears,
And, brother, for all time, hail and farewell!

IN THE summer of 1896 Beardsley made a set of eight full-page illustrations for the *Lysistrata* of Aristophanes. A limited privately printed edition was issued by Smithers but the drawings have not been published in England in their unexpurgated form. On the right, however, the frontispiece is now given in full, and above appears a detail from 'Two Athenian Women in Distress'.

The spirit of the play has been caught with true insight by the artist. Ribald and bawdily impudent, the illustrations have none of the prurience to be found in some earlier works; there is about them an air of maturity. Drawn without background, they were influenced by the Greek vases in the British Museum. Technically, they are superb, showing all Beardsley's mastery of his medium and sense of design; he described them as 'in a way the best things I have ever done'.

LYSISTRATA.

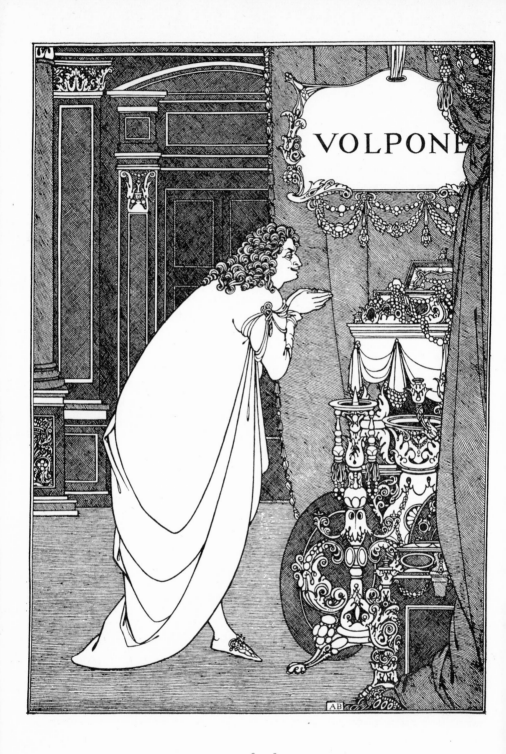

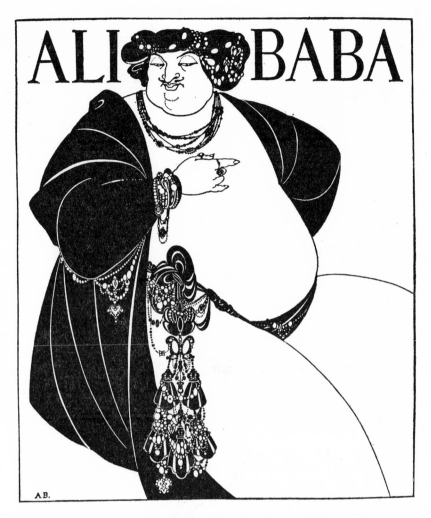

IN THE months preceding his death Beardsley, when not entirely incapacitated by his disease, was engaged in illustrating Ben Jonson's *Volpone*, and he died with the task incomplete. The design used as the frontispiece to the posthumous edition is shown on the left. All the former assurance of execution is there: it is a masterpiece from the hand of a dying man.

Beardsley made a number of remarkably successful designs for the covers of books. *Ali Baba*, above, was intended to be so used. The glitter of the jewels would have been even more catching to the eye when blocked in gold.

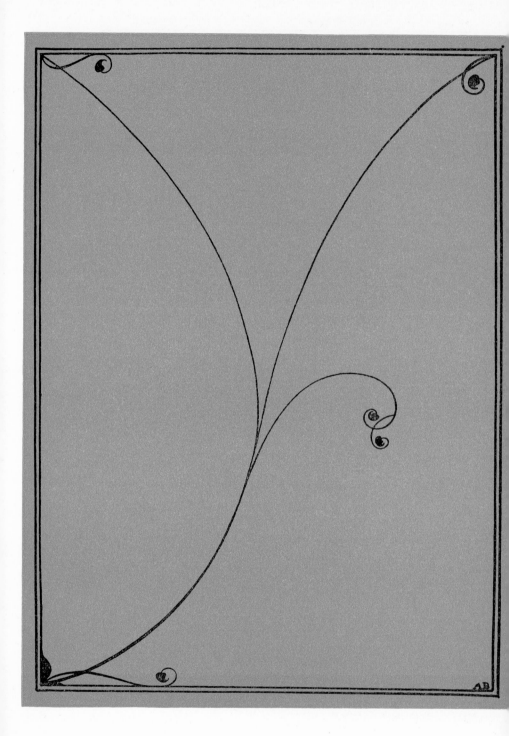

T WO MORE cover designs. The elegant curves on the left were drawn for Dowson's *Verses*, 1896, and the design above was for *The Houses of Sin* by Vincent O'Sullivan, 1897. Beardsley was an illustrative and decorative artist and his drawings were made to grace a page and to look well with print. It is by this standard that they should be judged; conceived in artificiality, depth and realism are wanting in them, and at times the artist's fertility of invention brought them near to over-elaboration; but as patterns in black and white, and in sheer technical mastery with pen and ink, they have not been surpassed.

Acknowledgements are made for permission to reproduce from Aubrey Beardsley's original drawings to R. A. Harari, Esq. (the drawings on pages 72 and 77), the Brighton Art Gallery (page 71), the Fogg Museum of Art, Grenville L. Winthrop Bequest, Harvard University (pages 63, 68 and 70), the Princeton University Library (page 78), the Tate Gallery (page 64) and the Victoria and Albert Museum (page 65).

A Pioneer of the Cinema

·⇶· OLIVE COOK ·⇷·

THE BIRTH of the cinema is usually associated with the two brothers Louis and Auguste Lumière and ascribed to a particular date, December 28, 1895, when the first performance of moving photographic pictures before a paying public was given at the Grand Café, Boulevard des Capucines, Paris. But the cinema was not the invention of the Lumières or of any one man. It was the culmination of experiments which had been going on throughout the nineteenth century ever since Dr. John Ayrton Paris had demonstrated with his pretty toy, the Thaumatrope, that a semblance of motion could be imparted to static picture sequences by means of the phenomenon known as 'persistence of vision'—the power of the retina to retain the impression of an object for a fraction of a second after its disappearance. Apart from the technical developments which led to the projection of motion pictures the history of the cinema goes back to classical antiquity when priests flung images of the gods upon clouds of incense with magic mirrors.

The supernatural element enters into nearly every attempt on a cultural rather than a scientific level to animate two-dimensional pictures. These attempts included, of course, the shadow shows of the Far East and of Turkey, and the Ombres Chinoises of the Chat Noir which were based on them, the great public spectacles of the eighteenth and early nineteenth centuries, the Eidophusikon, the Panorama and the Diorama, and every form of magic-lantern projection from the time of the invention of the lantern by Athanasius Kircher in the seventeenth century to the extraordinary entertainment of Robertson known as the Phantasmagoria and the immensely complicated shows of the Victorian period.

This dual ancestry of the cinemas in sober scientific experiment

and fantastic spectacle is reflected in the strangely divided personalities of many of those connected with its history. Kircher was a Jesuit priest and a distinguished mathematician at the Collegio Romano, but he used his projector to conjure up images of the devil and to daze and subdue a Whitsuntide congregation with a vision of the Ascension and an appearance of appropriate passages from the Scriptures upon the church wall. Loutherbourg, inventor of the Eidophusikon, a two-dimensional screen entertainment remarkable for its lighting effects and supported by sound, ended his days as a quack miracle worker. Robertson, the foremost exhibitor of the Phantas-magoria, was a professor of physics.

This duality of approach also characterises Robert Paul. He was not only one of the most important pioneers in the field of cinematography but he was the originator of an amazing project in which all the predecessors of the cinema, both techni-cal and cultural, and the film itself, were to be synthesised in one great optical experience. Paul was a distinguished scientist who is still remembered by the Cambridge Instrument Company for his brilliant inventions, and who is also known for the anti-aircraft height finder and the anti-submarine device he pro-duced during the First World War. At the same time he was gifted with a romantic and philosophical imagination.

One autumn day in 1894 two Greek showmen called at Paul's laboratory in Hatton Garden and asked him to make for them six copies of Edison's Kinetoscope. This peepshow for viewing moving pictures, which had been exhibited earlier that year in New York and also in London, was Paul's first contact with films. He was immediately interested in the possibilities of Edison's apparatus, but he felt sure that the American must have patented the machine in England. Much to his surprise it seemed that no such steps had been taken. Paul thereupon made not six but sixty Kinetoscopes, and exhibited them at Earl's Court.

The technique of throwing the tiny pictures shown in the Kinetoscope on to a screen had yet to be discovered, and Paul at once began work on a film camera and projector. This was the first step towards the realisation of a tremendous idea inspired by the Kinetoscope. Paul envisaged the projected film as part of a machine which would enable the spectators to move from the present into the past or future at will.

By an extraordinary coincidence H. G. Wells's novel, *The Time Machine*, was published during those very months, early in 1895, when the inventor was busy with his own concept of a Time Machine. Its hero, the Time Traveller, has made a machine which passes through time instead of space and journeys forward to the year 802,701. Although the writer could not possibly have seen a film show when he was at work on this novel, some of the descriptions might well relate to effects which are peculiarly those of the two-dimensional screen:

> I took the starting lever in one hand and the stopping one in the other, pressed the first and almost immediately the second. I seemed to reel; I felt a nightmare sensation of falling; and looking round, I saw the laboratory exactly as before. Had anything happened? For a moment I suspected that my intellect had tricked me. Then I noted the clock. A moment before, as it seemed, it had stood at a minute or so past ten; now it was nearly half past three.
>
> I drew a breath, set my teeth, gripped the starting lever with both hands and went off with a thud. The laboratory got hazy and went dark. Mrs Watchett came in and walked, apparently without seeing me, towards the garden door. I suppose it took her a minute or so to traverse the place, but to me she seemed to shoot across the room like a rocket. The night came like the turning out of a lamp, and in another moment came tomorrow. The laboratory grew faint and hazy, then fainter and even fainter. Tomorrow night came black, then day again, night again, day again, faster and faster still.

Paul was struck not only by the astonishing resemblance between the story and his own view of cinematography but by the fusion in the narrative of scientific and imaginative tendencies so close to his own. He wrote to Wells, and the two men met in Paul's laboratory to discuss the possibilities of manufacturing an actual Time Machine. The result of their collaboration was a patent application, No. 19984, dated October 24, 1895.

The purpose of the invention was to liberate men's minds from the eternal Now by means of illusion. For both men the Time Machine had a deep philosophical significance and was conceived as a means of probing the mysteries of the relationship between time and space. Paul was to be responsible for the mechanism and all the visual effects, Wells for a script which would prepare the audience for the experience of a journey into the Past or the Future.

Like the hero of Wells's novel the persons who stepped into Paul's Time Machine were to travel 'stopping ever and again in great strides of a thousand years or more, drawn by the mystery of the earth's fate, watching with a strange fascination the sun grow larger and duller in the westward sky, and the life of the old earth ebb away. At last more than thirty million years hence, the huge red-hot dome of the sun had come to obscure nearly a tenth part of the darkling heavens.' The sensation of voyaging upon a machine through time was to be conveyed firstly by seating the spectators on movable platforms over which currents of air were passed. Engine-driven cranks would impart a gentle rocking motion to the platforms, or, if desired, cause them to be carried bodily forwards or backwards. 'After the starting of the mechanism and a suitable period having elapsed, representing, say, a certain number of centuries, during which the platforms may be in darkness, or in alternations of darkness and dim light,' writes Paul, 'the mechanism may be slowed and a pause made at a given epoch, on which the scene upon the screen will gradually come into view of the spectators, increasing in size and distinctness from a small vista.'

Landscapes and inanimate objects were to be represented by means of lantern slides, and shifting slides were to show changing light and variations in weather, while films were to be used for living beings. Devices such as the cut-back and close-up, fade-in and fade-out were already, before ever the cinema existed, described by Robert Paul as essential components of his Time Machine. He also planned to incorporate a large number of powerful lanterns fitted with all the elaborate contrivances of the period, mounted on trolleys on rails so that images could be made to approach and recede and dissolve at will.

After the last scene is presented, I prefer to arrange that the spectators should be given the sensation of voyaging backwards from the last epoch to the present, or the present epoch may be supposed to have been accidentally passed and a past scene represented on the machine coming to a standstill, after which the impression of travelling forward again to the present epoch may be given, and the re-arrival notified by the representation on the screen of the place at which the exhibition is held, or some well known building which by the movement forward of the lantern can be made to increase gradually in size as if approaching the spectator.

The mysterious effects of total darkness alternating with dim light, and the employment of lanterns behind the screen, at once recall the technique of the Phantasmagoria, the Eidophusikon and the splendidly spectacular shadow shows of the Chat Noir, while the idea of the moving platform derives from the Diorama, in which the auditorium, a cylindrical room with a single opening in the wall like the proscenium of a theatre, slowly turned, moving the spectators from one part of a gigantic transparent picture to another. But the movement here was intentionally so gentle that it was imperceptible to the audience, who were under the impression that it was the picture which moved. Nevertheless the conception of a changing viewpoint combined with the movement of both image and spectators was not altogether new. It had been applied by the German artist Gropius in 1832, in his Pleorama.

Paul, however, did not wish to counterfeit reality with his Time Machine, to provide an experience which could be enjoyed in everyday life. The reaction for which he hoped was far removed from that of the painter David who on taking his pupils to see the Panorama in Paris cried, '*Vraiment, Messieurs, c'est ici qu'il faut venir pour étudier la nature!*' Nor was it Paul's aim to delude or terrify his audience with trick apparitions. He was trying to give a concrete demonstration of an abstract philosophy by means of a surreal art. He had grasped the peculiar potentialities of the two-dimensional image for presenting the purely fantastic and for preserving the fleeting moments of time.

The Time Machine never materialised, for Paul and Wells, both young men in 1895, were unable to raise the money to carry out their daring plan. Meanwhile Paul had perfected his film camera and projector and the 'Animatograph' as he called it was demonstrated on February 20, 1896, at the Finsbury Technical College, and on February 28 in the library of the Royal Institution, the audience on both occasions consisting entirely of scientists. The machine was fitted with a stand, the first of its

kind, specially designed to keep a moving object in view. Paul also built a film studio in Sydney Road, New Southgate, the design of which was copied for all subsequent film studios. It had a glass roof and sliding doors and was fully equipped for trick effects.

With the idea of eventually using all his resources to construct a Time Machine Paul began to make films of a purely topical character like those which Lumière had shown a month or two earlier in Paris. The subjects included *A Rough Sea at Dover, Whaling, Bootblack at work in a London Street,* and sporting events. Paul offered these with his projector to Augustus Harris as items in his variety programme at the Olympia. Harris rechristened the apparatus the 'Theatrograph' and after a triumphant run at the Olympia the entertainment was booked at the Alhambra, Leicester Square, where it was shown to enthusiastic audiences for four years. During this time Paul enlarged his programmes to include trick films and narrative sequences. One of his most popular films featured the Prince of Wales's horse Persimmon winning the Derby of 1896. It was projected at the Alhambra the evening after the race to the entire amazement of the public.

When Paul and Wells had set out to use the film in the service of the Time Machine they were free of the limitations which the cinema as an industrialised concern has since imposed on every creative mind associated with it. Ironically it was Robert Paul who, with the success of the Theatrograph, was responsible in England for transforming the moving picture from a scientific and imaginative invention into a mass entertainment. The films he made for variety hall programmes anticipated almost every technical device of the cinema of the future, while in content they complied with the taste of the audiences.

Paul realised from the first that a film is not a screen version of a stage drama but a visual spectacle composed of effects based on the incredible range of the cine-camera. Paul's trick films, unlike those of Méliès, his French contemporary, which show cleverly staged wizardries which could have been exhibited with equal effect in the theatre, have no existence outside the celluloid strip. Paul creates the catastrophic scene of a railway collision with the aid of miniature models; he exhibits a scene within a scene, two full-sized men watching mannikins in the boxing ring, by means of photomontage; cutting, montage and photoplay enable the hero and heroine of *The ? Motorist* to ride in their car to the moon and explore outer space; the same devices turn a man into a giant in *The Magic Sword*, a miracle which Méliès only accomplished by resorting to an enormous lay figure with meticulously articulated joints.

It was because of his technical accomplishment that Paul found himself drawn into the early film industry almost without realising it. His films and apparatus were in demand all over the country. He was usually required to project the films himself, and for at least two years, from 1896 until 1898, he would appear at four or five different variety halls in the course of a single week and often gave as many as four performances in one day. At the same time he was busy in his laboratory on new inventions and intent on improving his projector. Only now he perceived that all he had sought to achieve by mechanical expedients, platform rocking engines and sliding lanterns, could be contrived with the aid of the projector alone. By his efforts with the Theatrograph Paul had amassed sufficient capital to go forward with his plan.

But by this time the cinema was enslaved to the box office; it had been cheapened and narrowed to fit in with the typical variety show; it had already become a mass entertainment. Pathé in France and Messter in Germany as well as Paul himself and his followers, Hepworth, Smith and Williamson, had established it as one of the most lucrative of all industries. Charles Urban had started his career as one of the first and most important exploiters of the motion picture. The American producers, Laemmle, Goldwyn, Lasky and Zukor, had already appeared in the field; the new glamorous race of 'stars' had begun to emerge, headed by the comedian Max Linder. The moment for the launching of the Time Machine had gone for ever. It was utterly forgotten. In an access of disgust with the whole film medium, and the part he had played in promoting the industry, Paul destroyed practically all his films in 1912 and gave no further attention to the cinema.

Above: Paul's 'Animatograph' film projector, 1896, afterwards called the 'Theatrograph'. Below: frame from a film by Paul for use in the Kinetoscope or for projection.

ASSEMBLY ROOMS, CHELTENHAM.

PROGRAMME

OF THE

Cheltenham Cricket Club

CONCERT

AND

LIST OF PICTURES OF

PAUL'S THEATROGRAPH

(Animated Photographs).

TUESDAY, DECEMBER 1st, 1896, at Eight o'clock.

Patrons:

THE MAYOR (COLONEL ROGERS).

AGG-GARDNER, J. T., Esq., J.P.	GLADWYN, H. FAIN, Esq.	PAYNE, MAJOR SELWYN
BARING BINGHAM, W., Esq.	HATTERSLEY SMITH, REV. P. H.	ROBERTSON, J. L., Esq.
BEALE, MISS	HALL, J., Esq., C.E.	RONBY, REV. E. L.
BUTT, T. P. W., Esq.	HORLICK, J., Esq.	RUSSELL, COLONEL, M.P.
CREGOE-COLMORE, W. B., Esq.	KAY, SIR BROOK, BART.	SKILLICORNE, W. N., Esq., J.P.
DE FERRIERES, BARON	MELLERSH, W. H., Esq.	VASSAR-SMITH, R. V., Esq., J.P.
FRENEY, F., Esq., J.P.	NELSON-FOSTER, T., Esq., J.P.	WARD-HUMPHREYS, DR.

TICKETS 2/6 (Reserved), 1/-, Back Seats 6d.

Tickets may be obtained and Plan of Room may be seen at Woodward's Music Warehouse, Promenade, Cheltenham.

Frames from early films by Paul. Above: *The Bout*. Below: *The Phantom Ride*.

ove: *Her Brave Defender*. Below: *The Railway Collision*, 1898, for which miniature models were used.

Two frames from films by Méliès, Paul's French contemporary, showing his essentially theatrical approach. The giant in the lower scene, from *La Conquête du Pôle*, is an articulated lay figure which would have been just as effective on the stage.

In Paul's *The Magic Sword*, below, the giant has no existence outside the film: the effect is created by means of photomontage. Above: a frame from *Ora Pro Nobis*, which also makes use of trick effects peculiar to cinematography.

Paul's improved 'Animatograph' projector of 1904, the same in all essentials as modern cinematograph projectors; and four scenes from the film *The ? Motorist*, featuring a journey by car through outer space.

The Golden Age of the Bicycle

 EDWIN SMITH & OLIVE COOK

N 1791 the Comte de Sivrac astonished the public by riding through the gardens of the Palais-Royal astride a hobby horse on wheels which he propelled by thrusting at the ground with his feet. The Prince Regent rode a similar mount, and Dickens was a boneshaker enthusiast. But the Golden Age of the bicycle dawned during the 'nineties, when Mayfair and Belgravia took up cycling as a fashionable pastime and the morning bicycle parade in Hyde Park became one of the sights of London. The craze for bicycles was expressed by the invention of all kinds of odd machines: single giant wheels whose riders balanced precariously on top of them, or sat just over the hub, caged in by spokes, mammoth tricycles and fantastic 'sociables' upon which the sexes could take the air together. But the cycle ordinarily seen in the Park was the 'Safety'.

Its popularity owed much to the fact that it appealed to women. Although five intrepid ladies had ridden boneshakers in the first of all long-distance cycle races, held in November 1869 between Paris and Rouen, these crude, iron-tyred machines and their successors, the pennyfarthings, with seats nearly five feet from the ground, were pre-eminently mounts for men. The 'Safety' bicycle inaugurated a new freedom for women, symbolised by the baggy knickerbockers or short skirts worn for the exercise. As many women as men joined the recently formed cycling clubs, and droves of men and maidens, some of them seated on the 'tandem', bowled away on Sundays into the country, where their societies had put up notice-boards for their benefit. 'To Cyclists: This Hill is Dangerous.'

The cyclists of the 'nineties were the pioneers in the re-opening of roads which had lain deep in the peace of a fifty years' sleep since the coming of the railways. For a few—all too few—delightful years cyclists had the roads to themselves.

Above: the Railway Bicycle, manufactured in 1890 by the Kalamazoo Railway Supply Company. Instead of pneumatic tyres a continuous flat rubber band is attached to the tread of the wheels. An astonishing speed could be attained.

Below: a novel way of crossing the Channel

Left: a tricycle of the 1880's ridden by the Earl of Albemarle. Right: the Ordinary or Pennyfarthing bicycle introduced ca. 1870 and popular until ca. 1895. Below: Monocycle. Many attempts were made from 1868 to invent a satisfactory single-wheeled cycle, but, owing to the marked instability of such machines, without much practical success outside the circus and music hall

Members of the Melbourne
Ladies' Cycling Club, ca. 1895

Below: the winner of the
Scarborough Gymkhana, 18

The advent of the Safety Bicycle coincided with the Emergence of the New Woman, symbolised by tailor-made, mannish clothes and above all by knicker-bockers. Below is the heaviest cyclist of 1892, 'Baby' Grimes, in racing costume.

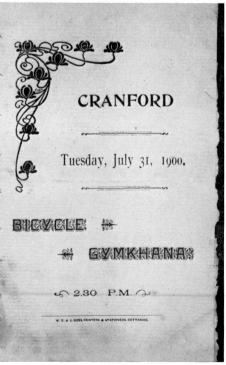

CRANFORD

Tuesday, July 31, 1900.

BICYCLE

GYMKHANA

2.30 P.M.

W. E. & J. GOSS, PRINTERS & STATIONERS, KETTERING.

A policeman's cycle, as used in some American cities in the 1890's, manufactured by the Davis Sewing Machine Co. from 1891

Below: 'World' machine, designed to carry five riders, ca. 1890, and a machine for three riders, ca. 1895

Variations on the theme of the 'bicycle made for two'. Above, left: Sociable, with separate seats side by side. Right: Jatho's Giant Sociable of 1890. The small steering wheel is under the control of the male rider. This machine was produced chiefly for circus and spectacular use. Below: a tandem tricycle of the 1880's.

Men's Cycle
Rally, London,
ca. 1900

Woodcut by
William Stra
'Cyclomania

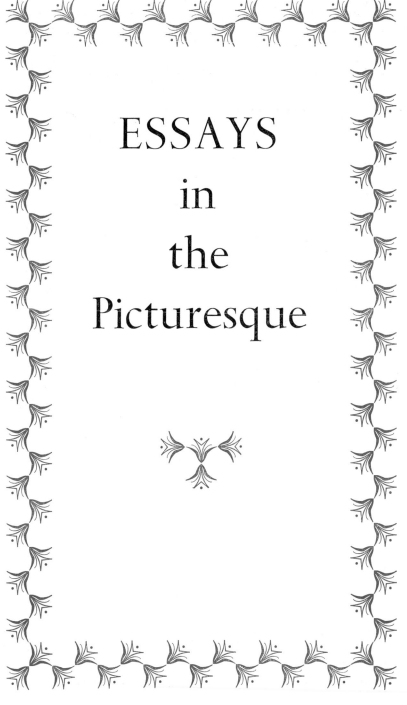

ESSAYS
in
the
Picturesque

Temples of Bangkok

PHOTOGRAPHS AND COMMENTARY BY

STEPHEN HARRISON

A S THEY FLY towards Bangkok over the widely spread rice-fields of the alluvial plain most people probably have little idea that the capital of Thailand ('the land of the free') will turn out to be the characterless sort of business city that they find when they drive in from the airport. Although there are some wide and pleasant avenues, the general effect is of sprawling confusion, with modern concrete buildings and neon signs superimposed on older shops, houses and gardens.

The trouble seems to be due to there never having been any over-all planning. When Bangkok was founded in 1782 on a bend of the river Chao Phraya, after the destruction by Burmese invaders of the old capital, there grew up in the region of the Royal Palace what is now a labyrinth of traffic-congested one-way streets. In the second half of the nineteenth century a new quarter based on what is still called the New Road was built much further downstream, and this is now getting slummy without being particularly picturesque. More recently, and at a considerable distance—not far from the Chulalongkorn University—yet another district has become fashionable and is being developed. The result is a population of more than a million and a half, spread over an area of some forty square miles.

There is no easily assimilable system of public transport, and this means, for the visitor, much expenditure of time and money on taxis. There are either the normal four-wheeled taxis (mostly Japanese) or three-wheeled two-cylinder open-sided vehicles—the successors to the rickshaw, but very noisy. (They are known onomatopoeically as *tuk-tuks*.)

All this must be rather different from the image of Bangkok in most Western minds, which is based largely, I suppose, on the musical play *The King and I*, and on descriptions of the famous Buddhist temples. These temples are, in fact, so scattered and, for the most part, so hidden away that anyone wishing to visit them on his own, and not in a conducted party, may have real difficulty in finding them. The maps which are available mark very few of them, and even then they will appear in many different spellings, according to what system of transliteration has been used. One for instance appears variously as Wat Suthat, Wat Suthas, Wat Sutat and Wat Sutas. (*Wat*, by the way, means either monastery or sacred precinct or a combination of both.)

To go by taxi is not the easy solution it may seem to be. It is no good trying to *tell* the driver where you want to go, for it seems impossible for the Western visitor to pronounce Thai names comprehensibly. It is advisable to get someone beforehand to write down the name of a temple in Thai characters, and then show it to the taxi-driver. But there still may be other snags to overcome. On one occasion I had shown a driver the written direction. The next thing was to settle the fare in advance, as Bangkok taxis do not employ taxi-meters. In this case I had been advised to pay fifteen *baht* (about five shillings), and I indicated this with my fingers. The driver counter-indicated twenty; but when I made as if to walk away he finally agreed to fifteen. It was only when he stopped the cab a few yards further on, and got a passer-by to read out for him the direction written on the paper, that I realised he had had no idea where I wanted to go.

Another time, having got over the preliminaries, as I thought, successfully, I set out for a rather obscure temple called Wat Rajabopitr, but the taxi-driver was convinced that I wanted to visit the Wat Benchamabopitr, a prominent and grandiose late nineteenth-century building, also known as the Marble Temple, which looks rather as if it might have been transplanted from Kensington. Indeed, he persisted in taking me there.

Once one reaches them, the temples are splendid havens of quiet, isolated from the noise and squalor of the rest of the city. They are mostly made up of a maze of buildings and courtyards, with *stupas* (bell-like shrines contaning relics) and *prangs* and *chedis* (slender spires and towers) spread out among formal gardens and flowering trees, the whole being generally surrounded by a high whitewashed wall. In most of the *Wats* monks are still living, and boys are still being taught in cloisters or under the shade of trees. It is pleasant to watch the monks washing and hanging up their so-called saffron robes (really anything from yellow to sealing-wax red), or to be engaged in conversation by shaven-headed youths wanting to improve their English.

If one is to appreciate the buildings one must be prepared for a profusion of styles and materials. Bangkok not having been founded until late in the eighteenth century, the most attractive temples date from then or the first half of the nineteenth century. Indian, Cambodian and Chinese influences were all at work, and the builders seem to have had no inhibitions. There is no austerity here. Ornately carved wood and stone surfaces may be left bare, but are more likely to be covered with bright paint, gold leaf or glittering glass mosaic, or even literally plastered with *appliqué* work, consisting mostly of bits of broken porcelain. Other surfaces may be covered with patterned tiles or inlaid with mother-of-pearl; and elaborately clipped ornamental shrubs are set in blue-and-white china pots among the huge figures of Guardians and grotesque mythical beasts. Above all, strings of bells tinkle in the breeze as they hang from the upturned gables.

In the bright sunshine of the dry season one's first impression is of a gaiety not unlike that of a Great Exhibition, though with more serenity. One wonders how on earth such flimsy charms have survived a hundred and fifty wet seasons, with their tropical storms.

One of the few temples which it is easy to find is that called after the Emerald Buddha, though the shrine in which this is housed forms only part of an immense complex known as the Wat Phra Keo. This lies alongside the Royal Palace, and the gleaming spires and pinnacles of both can be seen soaring above a long battlemented wall from the adjoining Phramane Ground (the main open space of the old city, used now for playing fields and a week-end open-air market).

I went there one sunny morning, having duly put on a tie and jacket, as instructed by the guide books. A man in uniform took the equivalent of a few shillings as I entered the gateway, and then I was free to wander where I wished, apparently quite

Chedi in many materials surround the central *prang* of the Wat Phra Keo, rising from the tiers of pointed, upturned gables.

Richly carved gables of the *bot* (main chapel) of the Wat Sutat, built during the first half of the nineteenth century.

Carved stone figures of early nineteenth-century European characters stand in niches along this colonnade in the Wat Sutat.

Detail of the side of the Shrine of the Emerald Buddha, built in 1784 by King Rama I, the founder of the present Royal Dynasty. The *appliqué* work on the left is done with bits of coloured porcelain.

Outside one of the many shrines in the Wat Phra
Keo. The gilded Kinaree—half human, half
bird—is a creature from Hindu mythology.

A carved stone figure of a Guardian, in the Chinese style, at the Wat Bovornives, which was built in the second quarter of the nineteenth century.

Window frames of carved wood and lions of carved stone against the white walls of the Wat Bovornives. The tree is, appropriately, a temple- or pagoda-tree (*Plumeria acuminata*).

Decorative figures of Giants, supporting a *chedi* (pagoda) in the Wat Phra Keo.

alone. As I approached the Shrine of the Emerald Buddha, however, I heard chanting inside, and saw that all round the base of the building were hundreds of pairs of black shoes, formed up with military precision. Returning there later, I found the owners of the shoes swarming out—smartly uniformed cadets of the Armed Forces Academy, who had been to their annual service in the shrine. A group of them, anxious to practise their English, soon surrounded the comic-looking camera-draped *farang* (foreigner, pronounced 'falang'); but these sophisticated young men were much too polite to use the slightly mocking term in front of me. In fact, two of them asked if they could accompany me. Having insisted on carrying my photographic equipment, they became my unpaid guides—though this is not perhaps the right word, as they themselves had never visited the temple before.

First we went into the Shrine itself, where the Emerald Buddha —in reality a small figure of green jasper—is perched high on a towering flight of gilded altars. I was surprised at the informal atmosphere. There were monks sitting about on cushions, chatting to some of the cadets who had stayed behind after the service; and some of the monks were smoking cigarettes. Later my two cadets—or 'Pre-cadets', as they called themselves—asked if I intended to go on to any other temple; and when I mentioned the Wat Po (known to tourists as the Temple of the Reclining Buddha) they asked if they could come with me. This was fortunate; for, although marked prominently on my map as occupying the next block and so only a short walk away, this temple turned out to be most elusive. Before we could find the entrance to it many enquiries had to be made by the cadets, now acting as interpreters as well as camera-carriers.

There were other sight-seers looking at the gigantic figure of the reclining Buddha (160 feet long), but they all seemed to be Thais. I was able to reflect that although the search for the temples in Bangkok was fraught with difficulties and frustrations, once I had reached them I had never encountered a single other Western tourist. Of how many other 'sights' in the world today, of such splendour and exotic magnificence, can this be said?

Low Country Landscap

ENGRAVINGS & TEXT BY GEORGE MACKLEY

F LAT COUNTRIES have nurtured some of the world's finest schools of landscape art. A land of strong horizontals is dominated by the skies, which assume great majesty and might and which, sweeping across the vast expanses, present a powerful drama of light, dark and movement. Moreover, any vertical that springs up from the general horizontality, though perhaps in itself of little consequence, acquires great power and significance in such a landscape. A sunlit building or tree, against the menacing darkness of an approaching storm, can impress us today as much as it did Rembrandt and Ruysdael three hundred years ago. But these mighty spectacles are not all that Holland has to offer. In its intriguing detail one finds pleasures of a more intimate kind.

For instance, hay, reeds and rushes play a prominent part in the life and economy of Genemuiden. There is, on the edge of the village, a street that is completely dominated by these products. Along one side of this street, extending the whole length of the place, is a continuous row of *hooi-bergen* in which they are stored. The *hooi-bergen*, though varying in detail, are all constructed on much the same principle. Usually square in plan, they have a pyramidal roof supported at each corner by a pole on which it can be raised or lowered. Anybody who sketches in Holland will discover why the roof is made to sit down fairly firmly on the hay below. The fierce wind with which one wrestles for the possession of the sketch book and control of the pen sweeps across miles of polders from the unseen sea beyond the distant dykes and would, if it could, tear the hay from the *hooi-bergen*, scattering it far and wide. The view along the street, with the parade of corner poles prodding the sky at varied angles and the pointed roofs tilting jauntily this way and that, is a fascinating one. The ladders leaning at yet another angle, the planks that flank the lower parts of the structures, and the carts drawn up alongside add further interest and provide the engraver with a variety of exciting subjects.

Cows are generally regarded as an acquiescent people and the cows of Giethoorn are no exception. The necessity of travelling to and from their pastures by boat seems not to disturb their equanimity, perhaps because the grocer, the milkman and all other traders have also to go about their business by boat. For Giethoorn has no roads. There are paths along which one may walk or cycle, but all transport has to use the many tree-lined waterways that intersect the village and connect it with the outside world. The canals are crossed by plank bridges or *vonders* which carry the paths to houses and farms. Many of the barns project over the waterway, thus providing a covered wharf where hay can be unloaded from boats and put into storage. The lively interplay of angles and tones in boats, buildings and trees incites pens and pencils to spring into action.

ALONG a tree-lined, brick-paved road on the top of a dyke
lies the hamlet of Eemdijk. The pattern of life changes
slowly here. Old traditions survive unselfconsciously
and not as a result of any arty-crafty or sentimental nostalgia.
A sketcher is regarded as inoffensive and is made welcome, but
anybody pointing a camera at the wearer of traditional costume
arouses indignation or resentment. The houses of Eemdijk are
neat and trim. Exteriors are hosed down regularly and paved
strips in front scrubbed until all is bright and clean as new.
Cleanliness and the adherence to traditional styles often make
old and new in Holland almost indistinguishable. The haybarns
of Eemdijk have been clad with corrugated iron and the roofs are
raised by winches, but, although lacking the mellow quality of
the thatched *hooi-bergen*, they have a beauty of their own.

IN THE FARMYARD at Diepenheim are three different structures for the storage of crops, all with movable roofs designed to give maximum protection. How old they are is a matter for conjecture, but all are built of rough-hewn timber, now well weathered. Their rugged appearance contrasts with the trim brick buildings behind them, but thatch is common to all. These brick barns, with their rounded doorways and part-tiled and part-thatched roofs, are of a type quite general in eastern Holland, where farms are built on set plans instead of having developed, as in England, according to the whim of successive generations of farmers. Even so, there is enough variety in the setting to make them individually interesting. The thatch, the hay, the timber, the brick and the tall willows, with their range of varied textures, present the engraver with an unusual opportunity.

IN THE EAST of Holland polder country gives way to forest
and heath, some of it reclaimed to form good pasture and
arable land. Here in places are gentle hills and there is even a
railway cutting. Through the pastures wind quietly flowing
streams, with enough fall to make it possible here and there to
work an undershot water mill. The mills are nearly all constructed of brick and timber and are often approached by way
of sandy lanes running under avenues of fine trees. The mills
themselves are usually surrounded by willows or tall and
mature oaks and elms. Many are double mills, one side for wood
sawing and the other for corn grinding, the wheel or wheels
being placed between them. Hobbema, it is said, worked here-
abouts, and this, no doubt, accounts for the sense of familiarity
experienced when one sees mills such as that at Diepenheim.

A BIRD'S-EYE VIEW of central Amsterdam reveals clearly
that it is built along a system of concentric semi-circular
canals. But those of us who are not birds can, nevertheless,
easily lose our way among the narrow streets and transverse
waterways if we leave these main canals to attempt a short cut
across the city. Most canals have a tree-lined road on either side,
each with a narrow footway, not very smoothly paved with
brick. To enjoy Amsterdam one has to manage to gaze at the
stately seventeenth-century façades with their stepped or bell-
shaped gables without either falling down any basement steps or
tripping over any *stoeps* or projecting sections of paving in front
of the houses. The main canals have brick bridges, but the
transverse waterways are often crossed by white-painted draw-
bridges which make a startling contrast against the dark trees
and shadowy water.

A Camera in the Clouds

These air-to-air photographs by Peter Warren, a young Ipswich photographer, capture something which even pilots find difficult to describe. Taken from a two-seater jet fighter they record the vastness and grandeur of the skies, the play of light on silver wings, the beauty of the clouds, and the three-dimensional freedom enjoyed by the pilots of Britain's fastest Lightning jet fighters. The picture above records a rendezvous in the sky as a Lightning refuels in mid-air from a Valiant tanker.

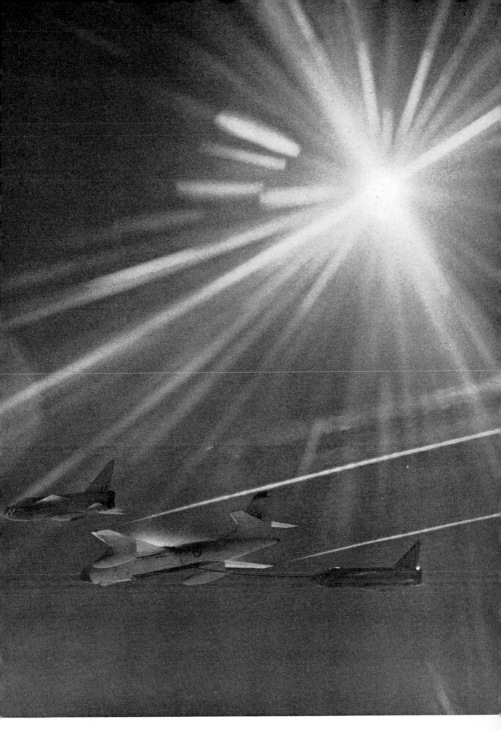

The blazing sun makes a remarkable lighting effect as Lightnings of No 56
Squadron carry out refuelling practice at 20,000 feet over the North Sea.
Left: Four Lightnings of No 111 Squadron—famed in previous years for its
Hunter aerobatic team, the Black Arrows—parade under a mackerel sky
with guardsman-like precision.

Pictures on these and the following two pages are dramatic views of the Firebirds aerobatic team of No 56 Squadron, which in 1963 was the premier R.A.F. team. A highlight of the Paris Air Show that year, it was the first team to use supersonic fighters, and these photographs, particularly the final one, show the high standard of perfection achieved.

Innsbruck

TUDOR EDWARDS

PHOTOGRAPHS BY GERTI DEUTSCH

The peaks of the mountains are covered with eternal snow. Water comes falling from a fearful height, and the cows, in the summer meadows, tinkle their bells. . . . There are millions of different bells: tiny harebells, big, black-purple mountain harebells, pale blue, hairy, strange creatures, blue and white Canterbury bells—then there's a great blue gentian, and flowers like monkey-musk. The Alpine roses are just over—and I believe we could find the edelweiss if we tried. Sometimes we drink with the mountain peasants in the Gasthaus, and dance a little.

So D. H. Lawrence wrote when he was staying in the Austrian Tyrol in 1912. His words express the essence of Tyrol. One sees again the high lost villages cushioned in snow from November until May, wrapped eternally, it seems, in silence, hanging between heaven and earth, remote as a dream. With May and June they are more accessible, and this is the time that the world of Alpine flora, emerging from its white woolly cocoon, is to be found beyond the stone-pines with their enormous resin-bearing cones. The earth is starred with white and lilac crocuses, and the slopes are stippled with anemones, the pale yellow auricula, and gentians of cerulean blue. Flax and primula creep over the rocks, and there is the perfume of saxifrage.

There are valleys that are far more secretive than the broad Zillertal, the Stubaital for instance, and the Wipptal that looks towards the Brenner Pass. From Mieders there is a steep descent to the monastery of Maria Waldrast, where one spends the clear cool night in a rough cell and drinks the monks' excellent lager before going on to the Waldrast Jöchl, a belvedere overlooking glacier and forest. High lonely chapels and calvaries reflect mountain piety and virtue as truly as the stoutly built rough-hewn homesteads reflect the spirit of Andreas Hofer.

Then one recalls days in the valley of the Inn, where, almost as regularly as milestones, a tortured wooden Christ hangs dejectedly on His cross, with, perhaps, a living halo of fresh meadow flowers added by a young girl. Ahead lies the complex of buildings of the abbey of Stams, a monastery of the Cistercians, tillers of the soil, whose vast walled estate and abbatial magnificence, rich library, and chapels screened with exquisite wrought-iron work, comes as an unexpected encounter. An old *Gasthof* near here has old-fashioned comforts, pinewood floors, and, in the *Weinstube*, one of the oldest ceilings in Tyrol. Here the fruit of the orchards and the wild strawberries were brought to table, so many years ago now, by Frau Speckbacher. Further along the Inn Valley, up towards the Fernpass, is Imst, where at the Spring Festival pagan rituals are reanimated every four years.

In the Otztal secretive villages cluster round the onion-shaped dome of the church. Some of these are archaic village kingdoms in a remote and ancient world, where life is reduced to elementals and there is no room for those who would be cosseted. Sturdy chalets and byres are of horizontal unsplit timbers, fir or larch, sometimes enriched with carving and pious inscriptions. Within there is evidence of a communal life and peasant art of singular interest, the latter in the hand-painted wardrobes and the finery of embroidered costume, and in the mastery of wood, beautifully shaped and polished, in utensils and implements. The Otztal meanders through a series of defiles and enclosed plateaux which ultimately culminate in Obergurgl on the very edge of the glacier and the polar wastes.

Such pleasures and diversions lie in the periphery of Innsbruck, that city of Maximilian, where the main streets are blocked by great walls reaching into the clouds. When that insidious caressing wind the *Föhn* blows down from the Alps it casts a spell on the people of Innsbruck, who put off all immediate tasks and duties and become inert. They are suffering from 'Föhn-Krankheit' or 'Föhn Disease. It was indeed in Innsbruck that scientists established an institute for research into the effects of the *Föhn* on the frail human frame and the unpredictable human mind.

Yet it cannot be said that Innsbruckers have lacked for vigour.

There are dynamic qualities both in their achievements and in their private lives, from the Emperor Maximilian to the remarkable Gumpp family of architects. Or should we begin with one of Maximilian's predecessors, the jovial Sigismund, who is said to have fathered forty illegitimate children? He it was who married the lovely Princess Eleanor, daughter of James I of Scotland, who left the royal arms of Scotland sculptured over a doorway in the Hofburg of what is now Italian Merano.

The Hofburg of Innsbruck, piled four-square about its courtyard, is of later vintage, for it was rebuilt under Maria Theresa, and with its rococo *Ofen* or porcelain stoves and the decorative paintings of the Riesensaal it is sheer Mozart. The most moving thing here is the painting of Maria Theresa's three children who did not survive childhood, and here they cavort innocently in Paradise, between the rococo sculptures and candle sconces.

The rococo, however, is found at its most capricious in the Helblinghaus, with its tiers of billowing windows and its carved human masks, birds, and foliage, and in the Landhaus, with its staircase turned into a painter's canvas by the Asam brothers.

Church-going in Innsbruck has its excitements. There is much in the Hofkirche, the former Court Church, but it is the memorial tomb of Maximilian (for which indeed the church was built) that lingers in the memory. A solemn mourning procession of forty royal ancestors was originally planned for the tomb, and twenty-eight of them were erected, all life-size and cast in bronze. Two of them, one of which is our own King Arthur (a symbol of chivalry even for Maximilian), are now attributed to Durer. Even by day they have a distracting quality, but given dusk this becomes a spectral arena, and one has the feeling that one has strayed into Madame Tussaud's. Strangely, Maximilian was not buried here after all, while Andreas Hofer, the black-bearded innkeeper turned guerilla fighter, was certainly not meant to be buried here but was.

The Jesuit Church is from the hand of Karl Fontaner and derives directly from the Gesù in Rome, while between them the Gumpp family built the Mariahilf Church, Wilten Abbey Church, the Spitalkirche, and the Johanneskirche. Wilten is a monastery of the white-habited Norbertines, and the church is a rococo efflorescence, but the parish church of Wilten carries this exuberance even further—its walls are of cream and gold and rose-pink, altars are like coral reefs, athletic angels strain from their cornices, and airborne *putti* swarm over all the furniture.

Back in the Altstadt or old town the narrow streets are pierced with round arched openings, and figures issue mysteriously from their dim cavernous mouths. These arcades or *Lauben* are characteristic of the town and are at their most sophisticated in the Herzog-Friedrich Strasse at the end of the Maria-Theresien Strasse. Here one is immediately confronted with the Goldene Dachl, which was added to the façade of the Fürstenberg as a sort of royal box from which the Court could see the pageants and the life of the street immediately below. The richly decorated Gothic oriel still retains its glistening sharply pitched roof tiled with over three thousand gilded copper plates. It must have smote the eye like a fireball in its pristine splendour.

The Goldene Dachl always brings to mind the Goldener Adler, which indeed is only round the corner, a felicitous hostelry with true regional décor, where I have repelled the biting cold with a draught of *Glühwein* or hot spiced red wine. It may be that more crowned heads have been pillowed in the 'Golden Eagle' than in any other inn in Europe, among them Gustav III of Sweden, Charles X of France, William IV of Prussia, Ludwig I of Bavaria, and the ex-Queen of Haiti. Andreas Hofer harangued the citizens from the window of his room there, Goethe and Heine dallied there, and Paganini left his name scratched on a window-pane. One does not, however, forget other wine taverns like the Leopoldstüberl and the Stiftskeller, or Schindler's, where one dawdles over *Kaffee mit Schlag*.

Above all, perhaps, one sees Innsbruck as a mountaineers' town. It is the seat of the Tyrolese Hochgebirgsschule (School of Mountaineering), and its shops purvey the ice-axes, pitons, and crampons made at Fulpmes in the Stubaital. Those softer of sinew can swing up by funicular and cable-car into the mountain world, and after there nursing the soul in solitude return to the junketings of the town. For this city of Maximilian offers the best of both worlds.

e Lauben, the Gothic arcades flanking the streets in the old town (the Altstadt)

The Goldene Dachl, added in 1525 to the façade of the Fürsten-
burg as a sort of royal box from which the Emperor and his
Court could view festivities in the street below.

Opposite: the Helblinghaus, rising out of the Lauben, near the
Goldener Adler inn.

In the Hofkirche is the tomb Maximilian designed for himself.
On top of a marble sarcophagus 'the last of the Knights' kneels
in his coronation robes.

The Hofburg, the imperial palace, originally built in 1400 but completely rebuilt by Maria Theresa between 1754 and 1777.

Overleaf are bronze figures of mourning ancestors, flanking the tomb in the Hofkirche where in fact the Emperor was never buried. The bronze knight is Count Albrecht of Hapsburg, inspired by a sketch of Dürer's.

The Inn va

n Mösern

Above: the Pfarrkirche, the parish church at Wilten.

Opposite: the park of Schloss Amras, scene of hunting parties as early as the eighth century, rebuilt by Ferdinand II of Tyrol in 1570 with the first monumental Renaissance hall north of the Alps.

Towards evening in the summer the benches beside the river
Inn are a favourite meeting place for the very old and the very
young of Innsbruck.

Up in the hills, at Imst, Spring is welcomed by an ancient pagan festival in which a dozen couples of honoured villagers are chosen to represent Winter (who is death and evil) and Spring (who is life and growth).

Extraordinarily bizarre and terrifying masks are worn by the village dancers who celebrate Spring in the Schemenlaufen at Imst. The figure opposite wears a skirt of corn-on-the-cob, large wooden bells round the waist, and a fantastic cone-shaped hat. The whole celebration is a flash-back to heathen mythology.

Rediscovery

The World
of John Tunnard

·≫ HERBERT READ ≪·

JOHN TUNNARD is an individualist. For more than thirty
years he has preferred to cut a path of his own through the
jungle of modern art. He began his career as a designer in
the textile industry, and textiles is a craft that imposes on the
artist a high degree of stylisation, even of abstraction. He had
further disciplinary experience as a teacher of design at the
Central School of Arts and Crafts in London. Then in 1930
Tunnard left London and moved to Cornwall, where together
with his wife he set up a workshop for hand-blocked printed
silks. As soon as he was settled in this new environment he
began to paint.

The style he then found has remained remarkably consistent
from the beginning, and even in technique and format there is
not much variation. It is possible that some of his characteristic

site : AFTERMATH
ache, 1962
Count T. Metternick,
*n

effects in the handling of colour were inspired by the silk-screen process, and there is even a suggestion of the threads of the loom in some of his compositions. From the beginning there was a mastery of oil, water-colour and gouache, but gouache remained his favoured medium and of this medium he has become one of the most skilled masters in England.

Tunnard immediately found a formal language of his own, and one that is not imitative or obviously related to the style of any of his immediate predecessors. It has some affinity to the early improvisations of Kandinsky (1911–15), and painters like André Masson, Miró and Matta may enter into comparison, for reasons which I shall try to explain, but this is because of similar intentions and is not a question of direct influence. There can be no doubt that Tunnard was inspired by the prevailing 'will to abstraction', but I believe his inspiration comes from a source somewhat unusual in modern art—nature.

It is well known that Tunnard is an expert naturalist—a lepidopterist, a botanist and life-long observer of all forms of animal and plant life. He has lived with nature as intimately as Gilbert White or Thoreau, and his painting is always related to the forms of nature—not so much to the outward forms, though these do sometimes appear as identifiable images, but rather to that inner morphology which is the secret of nature. By this I do not mean anything so obvious as the structure of organisms as revealed by science, but rather the formative principle itself, a grasp of which enables the artist to create forms that are analogous to those in nature. I do not know whether Tunnard is familiar with Goethe's theories of morphology (I do not claim more than a superficial knowledge of them myself), but in Goethe we find the distinction I wish to make.

'The German', says Goethe, 'has the word Gestalt to designate the complex of being of an actual organism. In using this term he ignores the factor of mobility; he assumes that a composite entity is precisely delimited and fixed. But when we examine whatever confronts us in the way of Gestalt, we find that nothing fixed, static, or precisely delineated occurs and that everything is in a ceaseless state of flux. . . . That which is formed is straight-away transformed again, and if we would to some degree arrive at a living intuition of nature, we must on our part remain forever mobile and plastic, according to her own example.'[1]

Tunnard is an artist who has acquired by observation a profound intuition of the workings of nature, and this enables him to imagine forms that represent the morphology of nature in its ceaseless state of flux. That intuition prevents the artist from becoming a mere manipulator of a lifeless geometry. His forms are the inventions of his imagination but that imagination is a complete world, in some sense a prophetic world. He himself has said that after he has painted a picture he will sometimes come across a form he has used without knowing that it existed in nature. This is credible because he works with a visual imagination that is familiar with archetypal forms—those universal patterns from which all particular forms evolve—forms which, as Goethe said, no Time or Force can destroy because they are born and reborn like living organisms:

> *und keine Zeit und Macht zerstueckelt*
> *gepraegte Form, die lebend sich entwickelt.*

And this is the sense of form that Tunnard possesses—not so much form as an objective reality but rather form as a prototype assuming an infinity of variations as the creative life force unfolds itself in time and space.

Paul Klee had a similar conception of art and certain similarities are to be found between Klee's paintings and Tunnard's, but Klee is more playful, more musical and immensely more prolific (and this distinction applies to another comparable artist, Joan Miró). I have already mentioned André Masson, and he perhaps provides the nearest parallel to John Tunnard. Masson is more humanistic (in the literal sense of often representing the human figure, which is absent from Tunnard's world) and more erotic, but he has the same sense of what he calls 'the secret world of analogy', that fraternity of natural forms which Baudelaire called *correspondences*.

'The grating of torn silk is like the cry of the knife in the bark of the oak—The adorable foam, thrown up by the ocean, filling,

---

1 *Goethe: Wisdom & Experience.* Translated by Hermann J. Weigand; 1949.

then overflowing, the high-heeled shoe of a woman; the voluptuous spiral of the smoke of a fire of vine in the summer air rejoins the endless trellis of dreams of abysses on the confines of the erotic'—how nearly these sentences from Masson's *Anatomy of my Universe* describe Tunnard's universe.

Masson's work (and his words) also suggest another aspect of Tunnard's work—what might be called its cosmic overtones. There is a drawing of Masson's which he calls 'The Unity of the Cosmos' and though this drawing is not particularly like any one painting of Tunnard's, the caption reads: 'There is nothing inanimate in the world: a correspondence exists between the *virtues* of minerals, plants, stars and animal bodies'—a perfect expression of the principle underlying Tunnard's art.

Virtues—that is perhaps the key-word to all this type of art; originally it meant 'the power or operative influence inherent in a supernatural or divine being' as embodied in a person or thing, and that is the sense in which we might speak of the forms in Tunnard's paintings. They extract a virtue from earth and sky and sea and all that has existence between them, and these embodied essences are composed into a dream landscape, a 'dream of a future desert'. If there is some suggestion of cosmic space, it is prophetic of the present popular interest in that subject. Tunnard's space is poetic, not scientific; or belongs to that super-reality where science and poetry are indistinguishable.

Tunnard is, of course, a surrealist if that word has any precise meaning. He has not actively participated in the Surrealist Movement as such, but if surrealism is to be defined, in the phrase of André Breton, as 'pure psychic automatism', then I know no artist who has more consistently practised surrealism. In comparison the automatism of a Dali or a Max Ernst seems 'contrived'. Much closer to Tunnard is a painter whom I have always considered the purest (if the word may be excused in this context) of the surrealists—Yves Tanguy. Tanguy's typical forms are more restricted—amoebic forms, or the cacti and dried bones of the desert—but nevertheless they belong to the morphology of the universe and there is a distinct similarity between the landscape disposition of the elements of the composition which both painters favour. There is also the same

[156]

BREAKWATER. Oil, 1946. *Coll. Mevrouw Roell, Bilthoven, Holland*

Above: STONE AND BONE. Gouache, 1955. *McRoberts & Tunnard Gallery*

Opposite, top: ENTOMOLOGIST'S EYE. Gouache, 1960. *Coll. Dr George Stevens, California*

Opposite, below: POISE. Oil, 1949. *McRoberts & Tunnard Gallery*

Below: SEA FLOWER. Gouache, 1955. *Coll. Mrs Charles Wrinch, Guernsey*

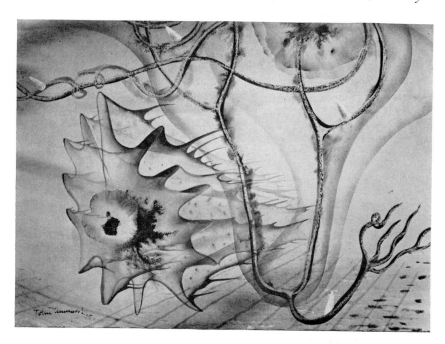

NIMBUS. Gouache, 1946. *C*

ott, Boughton House, Northants

NEW DAY. Oil, 1959. *Coll. Paul Stobart, Esq., London*

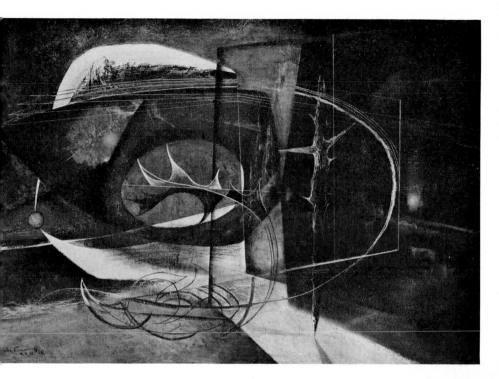

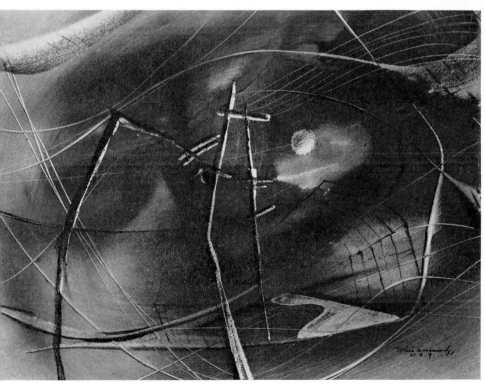

Above: RELEASE. Oil, 1960. *McRoberts & Tunnard Gallery, London*
Below: STORM. Gouache, 1955. *Molton Gallery, London*

suggestion of infinite space, Masson's 'dream of the future desert' Even their preferences for a modest format and for gouache as a medium give the two artists some degree of affinity. But Tunnards desert is not so prickly and leafless; it is not even the waste land—

> A heap of broken images, where the sun beats,
> And the dead tree gives no shelter, the cricket no relief,
> And the dry stone no sound of water . . .

It may be a sublunary landscape, but the images are intact, and their virtue is organic. Always in Tunnard's work, however *dislocated* they may be, the images have an essentially organic origin, and even when the painting is organised geometrically, with the fabric designer's precision, one is still aware of a vital process, of an implicit animism.

Animism and vitalism are similar concepts, and they imply a virtue which is more mechanical—dynamism. At times this characteristic in Tunnard's compositions threatens to disrupt the organic harmony—titles like 'Release', 'Flurry', 'Signal', 'Intersection', 'Flux', indicate geometrical lines of force rather than organic development. But nature, at least in its cosmic aspects, is also violent, and an art that did not reflect this fact would be too tame. The ideal is to find a synthesis of growth and form; but again, the forms that develop as living organisms.

The final effect is that of a dream-landscape, but 'land' must imply more than earth, and more than land and sea. The 'scape' is the limits of imaginative vision. Whatever the nature of the landscape, cosmic, telluric or, as often, submarine, the world created by this artist is a credible one. His work often reminds me of Sir Thomas Browne's *Garden of Cyrus*, where he speaks of those 'phantasmes of sleep, which often continueth praecogitations, making Cables of Cobwebbes and Wildernesses of handsome Groves'. Sir Thomas concludes: 'All things began in order, so shall they end, and so shall they begin again; according to the ordainer of order and mystical Mathematicks of the City of Heaven'. A painting by John Tunnard begins in the order of nature; it traverses the phantasms of the imagination; and then ends in the order of art, which is an analogy of the mystical mathematics of the City of Heaven.

osite, above :
ARTURE. Oil, 1957
. Mrs A. Kessler, Rutland
w : JOURNEY. Gouache, 1955
. Mrs Jane Davis, London

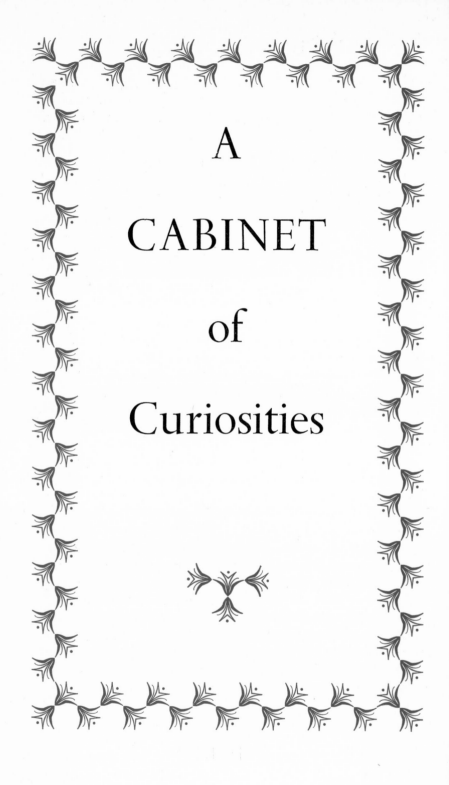

A

CABINET

of

Curiosities

A Slight Case of
DISARMAMENT

·❧ BERNARD DENVIR ❧·

SHAKESPEARE was not the first to note that 'outworn buried age' is especially vulnerable to the fell hand of time and mortal rage. Some six hundred years earlier Henri de Blois, brother of the Conqueror, had sent agents scurrying to Italy to secure specimens of antiquity 'in no matter what state'. By the seventeenth century, however, resignation about the ravages of history was hardening into acceptance. Within a few years of Shakespeare's death a Norwich doctor, Sir Thomas Browne, faced with the chipped fruits of local archaeological zeal, was busily engaged in clothing a contemplation of the inorganic victims of history in such a garment of hypnotic prose that material decrepitude soon become virtually the only outward sign of inner cultural sanctity. Ruins and the ruined cast an ineffable spell over minds and imaginations.

It is, of course, a good thing that we have learned to make a virtue out of necessity. The immortality of art has been hardly won. We talk of our classical heritage, little realising how few of its artifacts have survived in anything approaching their original form. Time and violence have played their part; the soil of the lands surrounding the Mediterranaean and the Adriatic is rich with stone heads, marble noses and terra-cotta hands. Often enough what we now look upon as the physical expression of Hellenic humanism is a hotchpotch of anatomical units each derived from a different source and matched together by the admittedly often superb skill of some eighteenth-century Italian restorer such as Cavaceppi—or even Canova.

But no sculptural surgeon, no matter how marvellous his powers of reconstruction, would ever dare to 'restore' the

most famous mutilation of all time. The Venus de Milo would be as improbable with arms as the Mona Lisa would be without a smile. The absence of the one and the presence of the other have become part of the folk-imagery of the twentieth century —a metaphor for sophisticated lyric writers—a stand-by for vaudeville comedians.

Devoid of colour, frozen in the sterile enticement of Parian marble, this mutilated Hellenistic statue, some two thousand years old, is still a more universally acceptable symbol of love and beauty than all her later rivals—aided though they are by all the devices of a technological, persuasion-conscious civilisation. She is, in fact, larger than life—though only slightly—her height is 6 feet 8 inches; her waist 32 inches, hips 38 inches, legs 48 inches. The distance between her breasts is exactly the same as the distance between them and her navel—a fact recorded not for any erotic reasons but because it proves that her creator was an archaiser, reverting as so many artists of the self-critical Hellenistic age did to older more certain standards of beauty and creation.

Yet, just because she has become so much of the stuff that our myths are made of, her identity as a work of art is obscure. Aesthetically—if there is reality in such arbitrary divisions of the processes of judgment—she may be faulted, but she will never be despised: never forgotten.

Milo—or, for those who prefer a more overtly Hellenistic spelling, Melos—is a small island in the Cyclades group, where, several thousand years ago, a form of sculpture was produced, and rediscovered in the late 1920's by Picasso and others, to become the progenitor of one of the more vital elements in contemporary art. The Turks knew the island by the less dulcet name of Bayuk Deirmenlick. In the winter of 1820, however, it had few, if any, claims to fame. There was one special point about it—expressed with what one has come to think of as peculiarly French fervour by the contempory author of an article in the then current edition of the *Grande Dictionnaire Universelle*. In the midst of a rather pessimistic account of the past history and current economic potential of the island, he suddenly bursts out into a panegyric about the women of Milo, whose great beauty—*admirables* is how he described them—obviously impressed him. They possess, he continues, *les traits, purs et fermes. Leurs yeux sont larges, et étincellent entre les longs cils noirs.*

It is doubtful whether Yogos Bottinis, a middle-aged peasant farmer of the island who lived with a miscellany of sons and nephews near Castro, had such ocular beauty, but his eyes were at least sharply efficient. On the morning of December 12, 1820, as he contemplated the bare, ungrateful earth which he was laboriously cultivating, they provided him with an immortality for which millions of others have sought in vain. His matlock struck into some hardness in the earth, and though others would have dismissed it as rock, he saw that it was something which had shape. It was in fact—as with the help of his son Antonio he carefully hacked away the covering soil—the roof of an underground crypt.

In a world where the past existed, as it still does, not in books or minds but beneath the tread of human feet—where grapes and olives grow out of the compost of history—this presaged wealth, riches. Men do not bury the valueless. War, catastrophe and death lead them to preserve the things they most value, for future enjoyment either in this world or the next. As the matlocks of these two peasants finally broke through, they penetrated not only into a kind of vault, but into time and eternity. Here, glimmering palely against the dank darkness, was the goddess whom we assume to be Venus.

We can never know what she looked like then, for she was absolutely intact—the first statue of her kind to survive without harm the ravages of time and the violence of man. Beside her, like two tutelary dwarfs, were much smaller figures of a woman and an old, gnome-like man.

From what violence of man she had been succoured, or what sight met the eyes of those who walled her up and then turned to face some monstrous reality, we shall never know. But she had been glimmering there serenely while the barbarians howled round the ruins of the world to which she belonged. The seas of Mahommedanism had flowed around her and left no trace. Men had lived and died in countless millions while she had preserved a more than virginal inviolability.

To Yogos Bottini she represented a dimension of experience with which he could hardly cope. Greed may have assailed him, but something else too—as he, Antonio and other male members of his household struggled along the stony tracks which led to the farm at Castro—a kind of awe, mingled with the angry realisation that to move nearly two tons of Parian marble even a short distance was a task demanding not only strength but ingenuity. The deployment of this last quality was in some ways unfortunate, for the Bottinis made two discoveries of which they took full and disastrous advantage. They discovered that the statue had been made of two superimposed blocks, and so decided to leave the base where it was and remove only the upper portion. They also found out—by dint of a kind of icono-clastic empiricism—that the left arm, which had been attached to the shoulder by an iron pin—was detachable.

It must have been their feeling of awe rather than mere commercial simplicity which impelled the Bottinis, once they had got what was by now the amputated figure of their goddess to their farm, to do nothing about it. There she stayed for several months uncomplainingly surrounded by all the bucolic squalor of an Adriatic small-holding. There too she might have stayed for ever—the working of that kind of peasant mind falls into patterns which elude our simpler urban analyses. But salvation came from an unlikely source.

Ensign Dumont d'Urville of the French Navy—representative of that fruitfully lost generation which had its corporate auto-biography written by de Musset, was not at first blush either a Hermes or a St. George, but his ultimate function as far as the imprisoned Venus was concerned turned out to be an admixture of both. Born in 1790 his parents had baptised him, with that careless passion for combining the sacred and the profane which is one of the glories of France, Jules Sébastien César, and feeling, perhaps with some reason, that after 1815 the marine forces of whatever dynasty happened to rule possessed a greater potential than its terrestrial ones, they entered him for the navy. Unjustly he is remembered as a footnote in geography not for having rescued Venus, but for having a tiny and geographically repel-lent island in the neighbourhood of the South Pole named after him, since he took part in a French expedition to those parts. Rising at an early age to the rank of Capitaine de Vaisseau, he commanded the ship which carried Charles X into exile, and then ruined his career by getting killed in a railway accident at Meudon.

In the winter of 1820 he knew nothing of these coming glories and tragedies. He had been appointed some months previously to the corvette *Chevrette*, commanded by Captain Matterer, which was engaged in making a hydrographic survey of the Mediterranean. That the restored Bourbons should be so passionately interested in these matters is an indication rather of their ambition than their idealism. Even an Alexander might have felt twinges of inadequacy had he been forced to succeed Napoleon, and none of the brothers of Louis Capet came within measuring distance of either the Greek or the Corsican. They were anxious therefore to secure land for France and territory for themselves in areas where any potential resentment would not take the forms which it had assumed amongst the Russians, English, Prussians and Spaniards on an earlier occasion. Captain Matterer, therefore, was engaged on a kind of exploratory reconaissance to discover those parts of the Middle East where his masters might secure the maximum of glory at the mimimum of cost. He was at this particular moment on his way to Constantinople where the Grand Turk was fulfilling his already well-established role as Europe's invalid.

The *Cevrette* was forced to put into Milo for water, and, as the barrels were being swung aboard, the young ensign heard gossip about the new resident in the Bottinis' farm. He was intrigued and went along to explore. Within a very short time he repeated the journey, this time in the company of his captain. Both of them realised that here was a notable discovery. Nothing like it had happened since the moment, two hundred and fifty years earlier, when a corps of Roman navvies had stumbled on the *Laocoon*. With remarkable presence of mind they allowed none of their enthusiasm to become apparent to those who were responsible for kindling it, and tentative questions by the now economically aroused Bottinis were anwered with evasive —though, of course, not entirely negative—replies.

Once the water barrels were aboard the commander and ensign of the Cevrette could hardly drive their vessel to Constantinople quickly enough. Algiers was still a dream in the future, Moscow a nightmare in the past, but France could now secure a sizeable chunk of cultural empire—and if she did that happy event would be not likely to impede the careers of either d'Urville or Matterer. And the man likely to help them do it was the ambassador of the Most Christian King to the Sublime Porte, Jean Marquis de Rivière (who was not yet aware that his new British colleague, then on the high seas, bore the significant name of Elgin).

Rivière immediately dispatched to Milo—with a large sum of money and a file of marines—his First Secretary, the Comte de Marcellus, who had acquired his cultural interests as Secretary to Chateaubriand during the period of the London exile. When he arrived at Milo, however, Marcellus—the name could hardly have been more appropriate—was confronted with an alarming and deplorable sight. Along the dusty pathway from the Bottinis' farm could be seen a confused crowd of peasants and *gendarmerie*—both Greek and Turkish—manhandling, with more vigour than discretion, the object of his mission.

To Venus abduction must have been an occupational hazard, but the Count, who after all came from a city which, nominally at least, had close links with the goddess, saw the situation as a personal affront. A sharp order, and the marines sprang into action, under the command of Commandant Robert. Blows were exchanged, a shot was fired; the spirit of Austerlitz and Ièna triumphed; the Greeks and the Turks fled. But the problem remained—would they return with reinforcements?

There was no time to lose. The upper portion of the goddess (there was no sign of the base) was manhandled along the road to the sea. Care was impossible. The arms were completely broken, and, though an attempt was made to collect the pieces, some were abandoned on the beach. Grave damage too had been done to the shoulders.

Once he had secured the more important position of his treasure, Marcellus set about seeking the rest. He discovered that it was on board a Turkish ship. Negotiations were opened, and, in the long run, by a mixture of bribery, eloquence and threats, were successful. A month later Venus was on the way to Marseilles and thence to Paris, a gift to Charles X from his hopeful ambassador at Constantinople.

Rivière had not exaggerated the pleasure which his gift was to give the king. The Bourbons had been lavishing a great deal of attention and money in making the Louvre as splendid as it had been in the heyday of Vivant-Denon, the André Malraux of Napoleon. The rearranged galleries, decorated by Gérard, Evaniste Fragonard and Fontaine, had recently seen the arrival of the Rubens Medici series from the Luxembourg, and a whole new series of Graeco-Roman and Egyptian antiquities purchased by the king from Tochon and Salt. The arrival of Venus seemed a direct sign of the benevolence of providence.

It was inevitable that attributions and stylistic analysis should tend to be over-optimistic. At some point between the discovery of the statue and its public display in the Louvre the plinth which supported the left foot was lost. Since this also recorded the fact that it was the work of 'Ages-or-Alex-andros, son of Henidos from the city of Antioch on the Meander', it was easy to infer that the sculptor responsible had been the inescapable Praxiteles.

It was not until 1893, when Furtwängler applied to the Venus an analytical eye unclouded by patriotic fervour, that it was generally accepted as a work of the second and not the fourth century B.C. Further research has shown that she derives from a fourth-century prototype, the Aphrodite of Capua, other incomplete variants being the head from Tralles at Vienna, the Venus of the Villa Athani, and the image on certain Corinthian coins.

The Romans made her into a victory by adding wings (examples are to be found in the Victory of Brescia and figures on the columns of Trojan and Marcus Aurelius). The combination of serenity, matronly dignity and sexual attractiveness, though they make for a certain stylistic lack of harmony, made the type a popular model for portraits of female members of the Imperial family.

Other details have emerged with the passage of time. Crystal-

line deposits on the neck and lobes of the ear reveal that she was once adorned with metal jewellery. Of greater interest perhaps is the fact that we can guess with some accuracy the position of her absent limbs. The missing plinth contained a hollow space into which a pillar could be fitted, and the fact that her left shoulder is raised indicates that her arm was resting on this pillar. Alternatively, instead of a pillar there might have been a statue of Eros, and her arm might have been around it—as in the case of a statuette found at Rhodes. With her right hand she was clearly holding the drapery which is slung loosely around her hips.

The apparition which had first appeared to the Bottinis was never to be seen again, and though that professional romantic, Ludwig of Bavaria, financed an expedition to Castro in 1836 all that it discovered was the outlines of the chapel where the goddess had been worshipped. Unfortunately she passed unnoticed by Pater in his peregrination of the Louvre, and she must remain contented with William Watson's more humdrum statement

And Milo's lurking marble smile remains.

Clearly however her popularity rests on a less literary foundation than that of her Florentine sister.

The Art of the Vinaigrette

·》 ERIC DELIEB 《·

PHOTOGRAPHS BY RAYMOND FORTT

T HE PREVENTION of the plague was a measure uppermost in the minds of men from very early times. The primitive physicians somehow stumbled on the fact that there was an apparent connection between the 'cure' of contagious diseases and certain strong-smelling aromatics. Thereafter few persons ventured into a house of sickness without some preparation containing various herbs, gums and spices. At first these anodynes were simply bunches of herbs, or posies of sweetly fragrant flowers. It has even been suggested that the practice, so popular in our own day, of taking flowers to the sick, originated from this conception. Gradually however, a whole range of elaborately devised containers emerged. A modification of these receptacles was the delightful and aptly named 'vinaigrette'.

The origin of aromatic vinegar as a prophylactic, or antidote against pestilence, began in sixteenth-century France, where, according to contemporary manuscripts, physicians were advised that 'a sponge dipped in vinegar and rose-water, or vinegar in which wormwood and rue had been boiled, was a sure preventative of the plague if the sponge were smelt often'. This early aromatic vinegar was compounded of fragrant quince, wormwood and other herbs, well macerated and allowed to stand.

With the advent of the seventeenth century the exquisitely costumed Stuart and Bourbon 'men of fashion' rejoiced in their splendid pomanders and other exotic compounds. The famous Goa Stone was a great favourite, and consisted of crushed gemstones reduced to powder, and comprising sapphires, rubies,

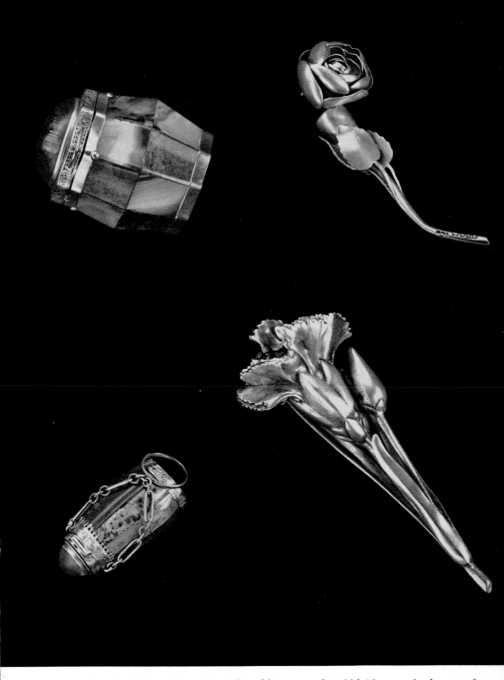

Some outstanding variations. Two Scottish gold-mounted 'pebble' boxes, the larger of 'octagonal section' comprising multi-coloured stone, with a moss-agate top, the smaller shaped as a reticule with 'carrying ring', both *circa* 1850. The two floral specimens are exceptionally rare: the smaller, a silver-gilt rose, has a tiny 'grille' set beneath the finely petalled head, and is by Henry William Dee, London, 1867; the larger carnation has a 'grille' hidden in one petal, and is by Edward H. Stockwell, London, 1878.

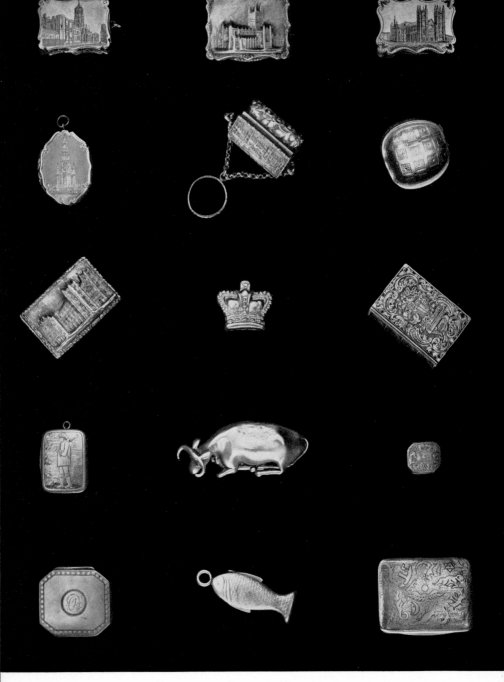

A varied group of *repoussé* and engraved subjects: with the solitary exception of the cow, all are by Birmingham makers. The three 'views' at the top are, left to right: Christ Church, Oxford, Nathaniel Mills, 1844, Wells Cathedral, Mills, 1843, Westminster Abbey, Edward Sawyer, 1844. Of the 'fanciful' subjects, the turtle, Matthew Linwood, 1807, the fish, Joseph Taylor, 1818, the crown, Joseph Willmore, 1820, and the cow, Henry Wilkinson & Co., Sheffield, 1834, are among the rarest of all vinaigrettes.

A selection of finely conceived examples: all eight specimens in the top three rows are of gold, and are, for the most part, of French or Swiss origin, *circa* 1780–1830. Especially noteworthy are the superb 'inlaid mosaic-top' box with a butterfly motif by A. J. Strachan, London, 1827, the silver-gilt agate 'scarab' with ruby eyes, *circa* 1840, and the French pinchbeck hurdy-gurdy, *circa* 1850. The silver-mounted cowrie-shell is another rare example, *circa* 1810.

emeralds and pearls, rendered with musk, ambergris and rose-water to form perfumed pellets. The more restrained Hano-verians used simple adaptations of contemporary 'patch-boxes' fitted with a 'grille' to prevent the astringent vinegar-essence (which was saturated into a sponge) from coming into contact with the skin.

When, towards the end of the century, improved methods of sanitation lessened the fear of contagion, the use of prophylaxis fell into disfavour. It is for this reason that few early eighteenth-century 'sponge-boxes' survive, although partially hall-marked examples dating from the 1740's have been noted. The renaissance of the 'sponge-box' (it was not known as a 'vinaigrette' until much later) came in the second half of the century, when fashion decreed tight-fitting costume and elaborate, towering coiffure. This trend, coupled with laxity of personal hygiene, made the use of restoratives imperative.

The ever industrious English and Continental silversmiths thereupon turned their inventive genius to the production of attractive containers, small enough to be carried about the person, yet possessing beauty and elegance. The vinaigrette of the now familiar box-type made its début in England during the 1780's, and fully hall-marked specimens by Birmingham makers appeared from about 1785, to be followed by London-produced examples some years later. The early prototype vinaigrette was a shallow rectangular container, gilded inside to prevent corrosion from the acid, and with a hinged lid and 'grille'. The mode of enrichment on the lid echoed the contem-porary infatuation with the 'Adam Motif', and was further enhanced by 'bright-cut' ornament (a method whereby a richly

---

Opposite are shown some exceptionally fine 'grilles'. Outstanding in this illustration are the flagship *Victory* amid laurel-wreaths, from a Nelson vinaigrette by John Shaw, Birmingham, 1805; the toxopholite example, which comes from the mosaic-top in the preceding group; the filigree in an Empire frame, by Linwood, a motif characteristic of this maker, 1816; the exquisitely pierced 'diaper-motif' from a Swiss 'quatrefoil' specimen, *circa* 1840; the magnificent multi-coloured enamel 'Forget-me-not' motif from a French amethyst-top box, *circa* 1800.

[181]

carved effect was achieved by gouging out the surface metal). Other plainer means of engraved embellishment were also employed.

Had the craftsmen been content merely to devise a utilitarian article, the story of the vinaigrette might have ended there; but in fact the evolution of this most charming and desirable bibelot was only just beginning. The realisation that it could become a popular item in milady's equipage undoubtedly stirred the imagination of some of the more adventurous silversmiths, and from the earliest years of the nineteenth century much thought and ingenuity went into its construction and decoration.

It is interesting to observe that from the very beginning an attempt was made to break away from the conventional 'box-like' types, while the function of the article would obviously remain the same. Matthew Linwood of Birmingham, perhaps the most imaginative vinaigrette-maker of all, introduced a series of finely conceived marine-animals—turtles and sea-snails as well as superbly chased scallops (with breathtakingly pierced 'fish' grilles) and finely wrought articulated fish—whose flowing curves lent themselves admirably to both compactness and 'clarity of line'. Linwood's commemorative specimens were also much admired, and included the famous engraved lid depicting the Hero of Trafalgar, in which Lord Nelson is shown in characteristic pose, the portrait being surmounted by his immortal 'Signal of the Day'. Other accomplished makers produced 'cast-top' vinaigrettes illustrating a variety of subjects, including finely modelled 'pastoral scenes', an outstanding portrait of Admiral Lord Collingwood, Nelson's great friend and contemporary, and—a very rare example—a classical bust of a Roman Matron crowned with a diadem.

The stress which has been placed on English specimens does not in any way detract from the outstanding French and Swiss fabrications. On the contrary, some of the finest of all vinaigrettes stemmed from the Continent. What is more, while the staid English craftsmen were content to work in silver, or at best in silver-gilt, the foreign makers delighted in creations of multi-coloured gold, enriched with glowing enamels and beautiful jewels. The 'grilles' of some Continental examples were miniature works of art in their own right.

The apotheosis of the English vinaigrette was attained during the mid-1830's with the introduction of the famous 'repoussé-top' specimens (the term indicates the use of thin sheets of silver hammered from the inside to present a reverse-image in high relief). These were mainly concerned with topographical views of famous Cathedrals, Castles and Country Houses, the accessibility of which was greatly broadened through the spread of the railway system, and souvenirs of which journeys were greatly in demand.

At this time the industry was in the process of being revolutionised by the great Nathaniel Mills of Birmingham. He introduced 'engine-turning' and other opulent modes of enrichment, and thus gradually transformed the flimsy little boxes into heavy-gauge articles possessing both beauty and utility; these innovations led to a general improvement in quality and style, although some of the earlier Victorian vinaigrettes tended to be somewhat clumsy. Fanciful as well as conventional variations were being produced, and from about 1870 a wide variety of sophisticated shapes were wrought, among them wonderfully cast and chased flowers, books, ships' lanterns, thistles, bellows, walnuts and cornucopia.

There is evidence that these superb little containers were as eagerly acquired in Victorian times as they are sought after today, with the obvious difference, of course, that they cost comparatively little in those far-off days, while some of the more important examples may fetch as much as £50 nowadays, and gold specimens are even more expensive.

The beautiful examples which illustrate this article have been selected from one of the world's premier collections, belonging to Mrs. Maria Hamilton Boss. To the far-seeing perspicacity of this charming lady the amateur of fine bijouterie owes a deep debt of gratitude. In seeking only the finest vinaigrettes she has afforded lovers of beauty an unparalleled opportunity to gaze upon the virtuosity of some of Europe's finest craftsmen.

The Social History of
THE QUACK

 AMORET & CHRISTOPHER SCOTT

L ADIES AND GENTLEMEN, may we invite you to accompany us upon a short historical tour, in which you will meet a few able practitioners of beyond-the-fringe medicine? And, if it is not satisfactory, ladies and gentlemen, your money will be refunded in *full* under our *personal* guarantee. And more. If you are not at the end of it convinced that there is more easy money to be made in duping the ever-credulous public than in anything you may be engaged in at present—well, read on.

Before we meet the first of our quacks, perhaps a few words on quacks in general might not be out of place. How the name arose is something of a mystery—probably it was from *quecksilber*. Mercury, as prescribed by a succession of German and (particularly) Dutch charlatans during the plague years preceding the Great Fire of London in 1666, was one of the earliest of fake cure-alls: and the date of the first use of the word, in its full form of 'quacksalver', is given by the *Oxford Dictionary* as 1659.

Why the quack flourished, and continues to, is easier to explain. The *British Medical Journal* put it well, if rather stiffly, when in 1911 it listed the following three reasons: 'The inherent tendency of human nature to delude itself; the failure of orthodox medicine to cure many diseases; and the dishonesty of the unscrupulous, who trade on the credulity of both the foolish and the wise.' These reasons are as cogent today as they have ever been. The weakness of human nature and the dishonesty of the unscrupulous we are all familiar with, but the failure of orthodox medicine is a sharper factor which is worth pursuing a little further.

[184]

In the eighteenth century, for example, orthodox medicine and quackery trod so closely on each other's heels that to the public they were often quite indistinguishable. The doctors relied very largely upon three methods of treatment—bleeding, dosing and enemas. If a patient failed to answer to the chosen cure, it was commonly stepped up until he did—or he died. In addition to their three blunt weapons against disease, many doctors and not a few amateur physicians had their own favourite remedies.

One such was the tar-water of George Berkeley, born in 1685 and later Bishop of Cloyne. His recipe was a quart of tar in a gallon of water, stirred, left to stand and the top liquid then decanted. This he recommended from wide experience as a cure for such varied complaints as Smallpox, Hysteria and the Bloody Flux. Another and earlier example was the sympathetic powder and ointment of Sir Kenelm Digby (1603–1665). The powder, reportedly 'brought from the East by a Friar', healed wounds merely by being applied to the victim's bloodstained clothing. The ointment produced the same result from being smeared on the weapon that had caused the damage. In each case, the wound itself received no treatment at all.

Now these gentlemen, Digby in the seventeenth and Berkeley in the eighteenth century, were not deliberate charlatans: Berkeley at least was a highly respected scholar and philosopher. But the gaping rents in medical knowledge, and particularly in diagnosis, encouraged such nonsense. And if such men as Berkeley could delude themselves to this extent, then the field was wide open to the professional quack. Small wonder that a sufferer would listen avidly to the smooth, persuasive talk of the quack doctor, who guaranteed a cure with his well-tried elixir, who pointed the righteous finger of scorn at the whole medical profession, and who produced half a dozen healthy people to swear that the only reason they were alive today was the power of the 'doctor's' miraculous draught.

One of these, born on the other side of the Atlantic in 1741, can serve as a model even today for apprentices in the art of quackery. Elisha Perkins was a genuine New England doctor with an undistinguished record, until he hit upon the idea of

putting to use the new and very largely misunderstood science
of electricity. His device was admirably simple—a pair of metal
rods about four inches long, almost certainly made of unadul-
terated iron, but reputed to be a complex alloy containing gold
and platinum. They looked much like a couple of polished,
headless nails. Users of Perkins's Metallic Tractors were instructed
to draw the rods gently over the affected part of the body,
always away from the centre and *never* in the reverse direction
(highly dangerous), for a specified time daily. The full period
of treatment might of course prove too much for a delicate
patient, in which case it was to be reduced. With this magically
simple formula, Perkins claimed to cure aches and pains, fevers
and debilities, and eventually to overcome paralysis and even
'deformities of all types'.

From 1796 until 1799 the Metallic Tractors were the rage of
American hypochondriacs. They sold at $10 the pair and made
their inventor a very rapid fortune. His success story would
have been longer, but he made the great mistake of diversifying
his talents. In 1799 he announced a new and infallible cure for
yellow fever, and seized the opportunity of demonstrating it
when an epidemic broke out in New York. Unhappily, his cure
was not infallible, and he died of the disease shortly after reaching the city.

How did Perkins succeed with so simple and so unlikely a
cure-all as his metallic tractors—and in Connecticut of all
states, where every cradle holds a businessman? He had a
presence, one of the prerequisites of a successful quack—he
was over six feet tall, good looking, and with a magnetic personality, according to contemporary descriptions. He had, or
cultivated, odd habits which convinced the public that they
were the manifestations of genius. He invariably slept for five
minutes after a consultation; never more, never less. His 'apparatus' relied upon principles of which everyone had heard but
nobody knew anything; and he used shrewd and clever sales
talk—the Tractors, for example, were sold at half price to the
medical profession (which had ungratefully struck him off in
1797), and were given free to the clergy. Poor Perkins. If he had
not meddled with yellow fever, he would have continued to

benefit from the world-wide success which his Tractors enjoyed in the hands of other promoters, including his son, for another decade. They arrived in England in 1799 and were, if possible, even more successful here than they had been in their native land.

The first quack in Britain to make a real financial success of the profession was Joshua Ward, who died in 1761. His fortune rested upon the simplest of supports. He had two medicines, the Drop and the Pill, and with them he could cure anything. He advertised widely, and received a vast amount of free publicity from the pro-Ward and anti-Ward wrangles which continuously broke out in the popular Press. He was on intimate terms with the most fashionable and influential figures in London, not excluding King George II himself, whom he cured (without either Drop or Pill) of a dislocated thumb. The Drop appears to have been a violent enema, the Pill an equally violent emetic (as one critic of Ward wrote in the *Grub Street Journal*, 'their operation was rough upwards and downwards'), and although not a few of his patients succumbed, more to the effects of the cures than the original maladies, Ward himself died of natural causes, an extremely rich man.

Perkins of the Metallic Tractors was by no means the only quack to make use of the mysteries of electricity. Indeed, some of his rivals made considerable fortunes from ideas far more extravagant than his. Probably the most famous quack of all time was John Graham, whose Temple of Health in the Adelphi, opened in 1780, housed the Celestial Bed. This superb concoction of luxury and magnetic hocus-pocus was in constant demand at fifty guineas a night. (It has been fully described, together with its inventor, in *The Saturday Book*, No. 16.)

Another electrical charlatan was Count Mattei, who at much the same time that Perkins was contracting yellow fever was doing extremely well in England with his celebrated and widely advertised specifics, Red, White and Green Electricity—each one in the easily stored and easily digestible form of a colourless liquid in a small bottle. Eventually someone sent samples of the three Electricities to the Public Analyst; Count Mattei was heard of no more when all three proved to be pure water.

In spite of this proof one could guarantee that Mattei left behind a number of perfectly honest people who swore that nothing ever again did their rheumatism (cataract, St. Vitus's Dance) half as much good as the Red (White, Green) Electricity. 'Quackery and the love of being quacked,' as Dr. John Brown observed, 'are in human nature as weeds are in our fields.' But some quack remedies really did make the patient feel better—for a time—whatever he might be suffering from.

A multitude of alcoholic cure-alls swept through the United States during the early nineteen-hundreds. Their sire, of about a century before, was Dr. Samuel Solomon's Balm of Gilead—a British concoction to the last drop of French brandy, its main (and, in fact, probably its sole) ingredient. Solomon's advertising literature claimed for his mixture even wider powers than usual. It could be used both internally and externally, and among the ills it was guaranteed to cure were yellow fever, sterility, horrors of the mind, debauchery, and shattered constitutions. The success of the Balm of Gilead can be gauged from the four hundred-odd agencies which the good Doctor eventually established in this country, together with a number in America and even further afield.

Towards the end of the nineteenth century, probably the most famous of the American alcoholic medicines—known as 'whisky tonics'—was Peruna, which contained 20 per cent of pure alcohol. So popular did it become that the United States Government was compelled to forbid its sale in Indian Territories, and to threaten that it would have to be sold under a liquor licence if the strength were not reduced drastically. The inventor obligingly cut down the alcohol content to 18 per cent, but this was considered not enough. After further pressure from the Authorities a small amount of senna was included, and this did the trick. Addicts found the effects so unpleasant that the story of Peruna came to an abrupt end—but not before it had turned its creator into a multi-millionaire.

Other tonics of the same era were even more powerful. Probably the king of them all when it came to sheer potency was Hostetters Celebrated Stomach Bitters. This concealed behind its innocent title nearly 40 per cent of alcohol.

It was only fair that America, which produced most of the men who tamed the strange forces of electricity and magnetism, should also suffer from most of the quacks who seized upon its possibilities. Electric corsets (innocent, of course, of the remotest connection with electricity) were one of their best-selling lines at the end of the nineteenth century, guaranteed as they were to put new life into the wearers, male or female. Electric rings were another profitable line. These, according to the advertisements, demonstrated quite spontaneously the power of the current (produced by the action of sweat upon the rare metals which made up the ring) which drew diseases from the body; for every few months a deposit had to be scraped from the inside of the ring. This, said the quacks, was the residue of the disease, forced from the body. But no, said the American Bureau of Chemistry, who analysed one of the rings; it was rust from the plain iron of which the ring was made.

More ambitious, more ludicrous, and even more successful, were the electrical miracles of Dr. Hercules Sanche, who enlivened the closing years of the nineteenth century with his Electropoise, which 'applies the needed amount of electrical force to the system, and by its thermal action places the body in condition to absorb oxygen through the lungs and its pores', which retailed at $10, and which proved to be made up of an empty length of iron piping, joined to a plain metal disc by a length of cord. This was succeeded by the Oxydonor, which was outwardly similar to the Electropoise. The price, however, was now $35, and the iron pipe held a stick of carbon. The patient was required to drop the pipe into a convenient source of water, such as a goldfish bowl, and sit tethered to it by means of the cord and disc attached to his wrist. Sanche went even further, by establishing an Owners Club, and a succession of accessories which could be attached to the original Oxydonor.

It will have been noticed that now and again somebody was unsporting enough to have one of the quack remedies analysed. The effects upon the subsequent sales of the nostrum depended upon who had initiated the enquiry, and how well the results were publicised. In 1909, and again in 1912, the British Medical Association itself made an enquiry into what it called 'Secret

M

Remedies', and published the results in booklet form. The 1909 publication sold well over a hundred thousand copies. Part of the motive behind the analyses and disclosures was undoubtedly professional pique, occasioned by advertisements like this one for a catarrh cure—'Have you taken all sorts of drugs and patent nostrums? Are you tired of paying big doctors' bills without being cured?'—and by the very large amount of money which such advertisements attracted. This particular cure, by the way, proved to contain the following ingredients on analysis: bicarbonate of soda; salt; borax, and a spot of carbolic acid. Cost of the tablets, one-twentieth of a penny. Sale price, one shilling. Profit margin after advertisement and packaging expenses, say, five thousand per cent. Another patent remedy which was analysed was found to consist entirely of pure sugar. It was sold as an infallible cure for whooping cough.

At much the same time as the B.M.A. was analysing quack medicines, the American Medical Association was amusing itself by conducting a correspondence with the proprietor of a heavily advertised slimming cure. The A.M.A.'s side of the exchange was brief, as follows: 'Dear Madam, please send me your new book that is free, and advise', signed with a suitably feminine name. This brought a succession of five letters (none of which the A.M.A. answered), expressing increasing surprise that the fat lady had not by now leaped at the chance of obtaining the cure, and dropping the price on each occasion. When the stuff finally arrived, it was a mixture of alcohol, alum, and water, and the inventor came up in court (the most usual hook to hang such a charge on was misuse of the mails).

Much nastier were the spurious Medical Institutes, which were merely ornate backgrounds to a psychological confidence trick. They flourished in the early years of the present century, mainly in the seaports of the United States. Their speciality was to persuade young men that they were suffering from one or more unmentionable diseases, further persuade them that by following their special course of treatment they could be cured; and by pressing on these two pedals at the appropriate moments, relieve the unfortunate 'patients' of every cent they could. There was eventually a public outcry about these establishments, and they were forcibly closed throughout the country.

Most quacks have turned from respectability to the border-line of the law. It is rare for the process to be in reverse; but it has happened. Certainly the most notable example of this was the rise of the Beecham Empire, now among the leaders in the pharmaceutical industry in this country. The original pills with their magic slogan 'worth a guinea a box' were the product of Thomas Beecham, and were made of soap, aloes and ginger, according to analysis. They were enormously advertised and highly successful, even though they appeared in that black list of the B.M.A. already mentioned, *Secret Remedies*. By 1913 the pills were being produced at the rate of a million a day. The admirable decision to establish the business on a more substantial footing appears to have been quite spontaneous—certainly there was no financial need with an estimated profit of about one thousand per cent per box of pills.

Does quackery still flourish today? Indeed it does—baldness cures (the only infallible preventative is castration), bust im-provers, rupture cures, smoking cures, drinking cures, lucky leprechauns, rejuvenating liquids. The claims are muted very largely, particularly in the case of cure-alls, because of the very necessary legal action which has been taken to prevent spurious claims for the cure of certain major diseases. But the regularity of the advertisements shows that there is still money to be made at the game.

And by the way in case you propose to take up our guarantee offer made in the first paragraph of this account, let us quote the reply of a quack organisation which made a similar guaran-tee and was asked to refund the cash sent. 'Your money', they said, 'is perfectly satisfactory, and we shall be keeping it.' How-ever carefully you read the small print, it's the other fellow who gets rich.

LOCKYERs PILL,

Call'd by the Name of

Pilula Radiis Solis Extracta:

O R,

The Univerfal Medicine, Obtain'd and Confirm'd by at leaft Forty Years Experience and Practice, both in *England*, and moft Foreign Parts (to be the only Solar, fingle and fingular Medicine) of the World.

Being the true and only Preparation of LIONEL LOCKYER, *Authoriz'd Phyfician and Chymift.*

THAT thou mayeft be certain that this Medicine is of an All-healing Virtue, the Operator, fince it hath pleas'd God to blefs his Philofophical Endeavours with the Acquifition and true Perfection thereof, has Adminiftred and Experimented the fame with Succefs upon All or Moft Part of the known Difeafes and Diftempers of Man (both Internal and External) of all Sorts of Perfons, of all Conftitutions and Complexions, of all Ages, reducing all the afflicted Parts of the Body, to their proper Natural Function, Motion, and Order; having in it the Vertues and Quinteffence of all Medicines: No Perfon having yet ever fail'd of Cure, who has continued (without Intermiffion, or Inter-mixture of other Phyfick) to the true Method of ufing this Medicine. ·

But for the more exact and punctual Satisfaction of all Perfons, here is a particular Account of the feveral Difeafes that have been abfolutely Cured by this ONE MEDICINE, and to be Attefted by the Experience of feveral Parties fo Cured, viz.

The Falling-Sicknefs, Frenzy, Vertigo, Rheums or Defluxions, Head-ach of all Kinds, Convulfion-Fits. Difficulty of Breathing, Stoppage of the Stomach, Cough, Tiffick, Inflammation of the Lungs, Confumption. Want of Appetite, bad Digeftion, Pain in the Stomach. Worms of all Kinds, Colick. Inflammations and Obftructions of the Liver, Corruption, Putrefaction of the Blood,Jaundies, Black and Yellow; Dropfie or Tympany, Hard Swellings,Pain and Inflammations of the Spleen, Overflowing of the Gall. Trembling of the Heart, Swoonings. Stoppage and Scalding of Urine, Bloody-Flux, Gravel and Stone in the Reins and Bladder. Rickets in Children. King's Evil, Tumours and Hard Swellings,and Ulcers on the Body, Leprofie, Scurvy, Scab, Itch, &c. The *Gonorrhœa*, or Running of the Reins ; The POX, the Gout, Violent and Hectick Fevers, Agues, Quotidian, Tertian, Quartan ; Green-Sicknefs,Fits of the Mother, Stoppage of Terms, &c.

ALSO,

It highly reftores the Radical Moifture, cleanfes and ftrengthens the Spermatick Veffels, increafes and animates the Seed in both Sexes, fortifies the Womb, preferves the Embryo, ftrengthens the Child, and prevents Mifcarriage, reftores the loft Delight of Nature, and abfolutely cures all Barrennefs curable by Medicine: It is alfo an Antidote againft all Contagious Airs, and Infectious Difeafes ; and perfectly refifts all Foulnefs and Infection in the Act of Generation. It mundifies and cleanfes the Skin, reftores and increafes Beauty, makes Old Age Comely and Beautiful, and the Countenance of all to be Chearful and Sanguine.

Since the Deceafe of the Doctor, as his BOOK directs, Thefe PILLS are made up in Tin Boxes being about an Hundred in Number, Price 4 *s.* and about Fifty in the Half-Box, Price 2 *s.* and (to prevent your being abus'd with Counterfeits) Lapt up in Papers, wherein are the Names of *Thomas Fyge* and *John Watts*, his Nominees for this Secret written with our own Hands, and Sealed at one End, with the Doctor's Coat of Arms, being Three Boars-Heads, and at the other, with the Arms of the faid *Tho. Fyge*, being Six Flower-de-luces and Three Spur Rowels ; And no where to be had by Wholefale, but from the Daughters of Mr. *Tho. Fyge*, Apothecary, at the *Sugar-Loaf* without *Bifhopfgate*, *John Watts* junior, in *Racket Court* in *Fleetftreet*, and *John Watts* fenior (Nephew and Operator to the Doctor at the time of his Death) in S. *Thomas's Southwark.* There are two Lions on the Poft at the Door, each holding a Shield, on which are painted Three Boars-Heads, and is the Dwelling Houfe in which lived and died Dr. *LOCKYER.*

At which Places, any Perfon may be furnifh'd with the true PILL, with Allowance for Encouragement of the Sale thereof, in any Town or City of *Great Brittain* or *Ireland*, where the fame are not already fold.

They are alfo fold by Retail, in feveral Cities in *England*, and particularly by Mr. *Florne*, Bookfeller, and Mrs. *Garraway*, Fruiterer, both under the South-Gate of the *Royal-Exchange*, LONDON.

A Troupe of Puppets

GEORGE SPEAIGHT

AMONG the early memories of almost every English child is a little red and yellow hunchback banging his stick on to his wife's head and screaming in a peculiar nasal screech, 'That's the way to do it.' Or it may be a memory of the romantic landscapes of toy theatre scenery, with flat cardboard characters declaiming heroic sentiments; or of the contrived, deliberate movements of a wooden puppet in a marionette show at a children's party. Punch and Judy, toy theatres, and marionettes are part of our tradition of childhood. Sometimes the early memory is a seed that flowers into a lifelong passion. It was so with me.

As I grew older I learnt that in other countries there were other puppet heroes: Guignol in France, Kasperl in Germany, Tchantchès in Liège, Hänneschen in Cologne, Gianduja in Turin, Gerolamo in Milan, Faggiolino in Bologna, Facanapa in Venice, Pulcinella in Naples, Karaguez in Greece, and many another. I learnt, too, that there were many kinds of puppets: glove puppets that fit on the hand, rod puppets worked from under the stage, marionettes worked from above the stage, shadow figures that are translucent and shadow figures that are opaque, three puppets worked by one man and one puppet worked by three men, and so on. I learnt that there were many kinds of puppet shows: folk plays for peasants and slapstick for children; Christian epics and Hindu epics; sagas of war and sagas of love; poetry in artists' studios and satire in political cabarets; fantasy for princes and opera for cardinals; expressionist, surrealist, abstract puppets; romantic, naturalistic, beautiful puppets.

I began to read books about puppets, and even wrote a history of them myself. I collected examples of puppet literature from other countries (I must have almost two dozen languages represented on my shelves); I collected early playbills and prints and pictures of puppets. And, at home and abroad, in junk shops and antique shops and open markets and in the backstage of

[193]

theatres, I searched for old and interesting puppets themselves.

'Would you be interested in buying some old puppets?' The collector of puppets learns to receive such enquiries with a proper mixture of enthusiasm and caution. So often they turn out to be not old at all, or not puppets at all—dolls or artists' lay figures. Usually the seller says they are Italian (I recall with pleasure my delight at being able to inform one such would-be seller that the figures he offered were not only not Italian but were made by an English puppeteer whom I could name!). But one cannot afford to turn any possibility away, and so it was that one bleak winter day just after the end of the war found me travelling to the pleasant Lincolnshire country town of Spalding (which is justly noted for the library of its Gentlemen's Society). The familiar enquiry had come to a friend of mine, Mr Gerald Morice, who has performed the remarkable journalistic feat of contributing for over 25 years a weekly column of 'Puppet Pars' to that fascinating journal of fairground and circus entertainers, *The World's Fair*. Mr Morice was abroad, administering the ex-enemies in Europe. Would I look at these puppets? I would.

From Spalding I took a bus through the flat Dutch landscape to a near-by village. Enquiry led me to the cottage where lived the lady who had written the letter. Would I like to see the puppets? Of course. They were in a barn down a lane. We went down a farm track and into the barn. At one end stood three huge boxes. My nostrils quivered. The boxes were thrown open and their contents revealed.

It was the entire troupe of a Victorian marionette theatre, over fifty figures; each some two and a half feet high, carved from wood, painted and dressed. There were the stock characters for any melodrama: heroines in neat print dresses, heroes in honest working men's shirts and breeches, bereaved widows in mourning weeds, smooth villains in frock coats; there was the comic character who popped up in every play, Tim Bobbin, a rustic yokel who had evolved from Lancashire folklore; there were the pantomime characters: Harlequin with a moustache, Columbine with well-developed calves, Pantaloon and Clown; there were the characters who sprang from the circus: the juggler who caught balls on his toes, the antipodist who juggled with his feet, the Blondin who walked the tight-rope, and the stilt walkers; and there were the *fantoccini*, the figures of fancy: the Scaramouch with three heads, the two Cures (so named after a once popular music-hall song of the 'sixties) who could shrink to the size of midgets or shoot up to the height of giants, and the skeleton whose bones floated apart and then came together again.

Shows like this had travelled round England, and round Europe and America, for centuries. They were usually family affairs, carving their own figures, dressing them, stringing them, adapting their own plays, and performing them night after night in a wide repertory of folk tales, popular melodramas and pantomimes. They were always on the move, setting up on a village green or in a fair for a week or so, and then taking the booth down, loading it on the waggons and on to the next stop. This one dated back to the mid-nineteenth century, though it drew on much older traditions; it had been created from a union between the Tiller and Clowes families—families with wide ramifications among the nineteenth-century English marionette showmen. It had been caught by the outbreak of the Great War in 1914 in this little village; the men had joined up, the women had settled to work on the land, and the puppets and scenery had been stored away in this barn. They had never been looked at since. After the war some of the men had not come back, and others were restless beneath the iron discipline of their father, the master of the show; besides, the cinema was the thing now, and few people had much time for an old-fashioned marionette theatre. The boxes had lain there unopened till I came to see them over thirty years later.

The show was bought. No other answer was possible. It was a fantastic, an almost unique discovery. Merely as collector's pieces the figures were examples of an art and craft of which few examples have survived. But must they remain mere objects of display? Could they be given life? Could they perform again? The possibility suggested a way of recouping the purchase price.

For some years nothing was done. And then a conjunction of circumstances made our dream a possibility. The firm for which I worked went into liquidation, leaving me out of a job; my aunt died, leaving me enough money to live on for a year or so; and the government decided to hold a Festival of Britain, to commemorate the centenary of the Great Exhibition, in 1951. As part of the Festival of Britain there were to be the Festival Pleasure Gardens in Battersea Park, to provide what a Minister described as 'the slap and tickle' element in the festivities. As part of the Festival Pleasure Gardens there was to be the Riverside Theatre, to introduce a note of light-hearted culture into the slap and tickle; and as part of the repertory of the Riverside Theatre there were to be puppet shows every afternoon, where exhausted slappers and ticklers could take their children and sit down. So the Gardens were looking out for suitable puppet shows; Gerald Morice and I offered to put on a Victorian marionette show with the title of The Old Time Marionettes; and Jack Carlton, the Gardens' entertainment manager—with no little faith in a quite untried experiment—accepted our offer. We got a month's contract, to the considerable annoyance of several English puppeteers who had established shows of their own and who doubted the capacity of a couple of impractical intellectuals to put on one for themselves.

We now found ourselves with a contract, due to start in three months' time, but with no show. Three boxes of old, dishevelled marionettes do not constitute a puppet theatre capable of performances in public. However, we set to work with vigour and enthusiasm: we undressed the puppets and washed their clothes, and our wives and mothers exclaimed at the fineness of their materials as they ironed them and mended them where required; we cleaned the puppets, and no picture restorer at the National Gallery could have removed the dirt of the years with more care, nor have watched with more enthusiasm the original paint coming up as bright as on the day it was put on. We cut away the old strings, which were hopelessly tangled and rotted, and re-strung the figures on the original two-bar controls.

As these hundred-year-old marionettes once again moved their limbs in answer to the guiding strings I felt that I was indeed bringing the past to life. No archaeologist reconstructing an ancient civilisation could have felt a greater thrill than I did as I teased out the mysteries of stringing and control which

The author backstage with some of the Victorian marionettes that he restored to working order, and which were presented during the Festival of Britain as The Old Time Marionettes. From left to right in the front row are Tim Bobbin, a factory girl, a miner in the Australian gold rush, a cad, a nigger minstrel and Tommy, an old sailor and street fiddler.

Some *fantoccini* figures hanging in the wings. From left to right (front row) are Columbine, Chinese antipodist with cylinder (which he juggles with his feet), Joey (clown), ball juggler, and Blondin (tight-rope walker); (back row) stiltwalking clown, policeman, Pantaloon, the two Curés (with expanding and contracting bodies) and Tim Bobbin (Lancashire folk character). These were all traditional types of the nineteenth-century English puppet theatres.

Left: Pantaloon, a character who entered English pantomime from the *commedia dell' arte*.

The lover, the daughter and the father. Characters from the ballad of 'Villikins and Dinah'.

Pantaloon, Harlequin, Columbine and Clown in the Harlequinade Ballet, specially arranged for The Old Time Marionettes to the music of Sullivan.

The juggler throws two balls into the air, catching one on his foot and the other on his head. The secret lies in the ingenious method of stringing.

generations of puppet showman had guarded as the secrets of their profession.

At last some forty puppets were restored and in working order. We planned a programme of old music-hall songs, traditional tricks, and a harlequinade ballet to Sullivan's music. Reginald Woolley, of the Players' Theatre, painted some new scenery. We engaged experienced marionette manipulators and singers to assist us. I hardly slept or ate for the last week of rehearsals. We drove, in period costume, through the streets of London in a picturesque horse cart on our way to the Gardens. And on the day, the curtain rose on our mad, hare-brained venture as Tim Bobbin stepped forward with the words of the prologue I had composed for him:

> I'm a Lancashire lad, Tim Bobbin by name,
> And to see the famed wonders of London I came.
> The Festival shows I wanted to see
> And 'the slap and the tickle' at this Battersea.
> But when at the gate I was all ready set
> They said, 'Go away. We're not open yet.'[1]
> And so down the river I presently went
> To see those famed Houses of Parliament,
> Where they put on more taxes day after day,
> And expect poor Bobbins like me to pay.
> At first I couldn't see where they were,
> But then, all at once, sticking up in the air,
> All shining and bright, I saw Churchill's cigar[2]
> To show where the Houses of Parliament are.

The audiences were gratifyingly large, but I don't know if the performance was a good one. Critics did not visit the Riverside Theatre. The resurrection story of the old marionette theatre, which seemed so romantic to me, raised barely a flutter of interest in Fleet Street. We worked the publicity for all it was worth, but nobody who mattered came out to Battersea; the B.B.C., the Arts Council, the British Council, the Edinburgh Festival were all 'too busy'. No matter. It was a lovely August.

1 An allusion to delays in completing the Festival Gardens, which opened late.
2 An allusion to the Skylon, a large torpedo-shaped object, the emblem of the Festival of Britain, which was floodlit at night.

In one's memory, it never rained. For a few brief weeks, before economic stringency and political prejudice had their way, Londoners could again drink beer and wine beneath the trees, and listen to the band, gaze at the fireworks down the fountain vista, and watch the puppets beside the flowing Thames.

The Old Time Marionettes certainly never made our fortunes, though I suppose they recouped their purchase price. They only gave one further season, when, a few years later, they performed as a pre-Christmas entertainment at Heal's Toy Fair. I sometimes demonstrate them at lectures, but it will need some coaxing to persuade them to play before the footlights again.

Perhaps the discovery and renovating of this old theatre may have done something to make the traditional English marionette theatre more widely known and appreciated. Indeed, among the English popular arts the marionettes should hold a high place. With the primitive vigour of their carving and the theatrical panache of their costumes they take their place beside the ships' figure-heads and the galloping horses on fairground roundabouts, while the naïve charm of their scenery belongs to the romantic world of twopence-coloured toy theatres and painted castles on narrow boats. Their stilted, somewhat rheumatic movements invest them with the gravity of walking statues. Their impassive, mask-like countenances invite our imaginations to give them life.

The history of puppets provides many examples of a primitive folk art with deep roots in native folklore. In China, Japan and Indonesia magnificant examples still survive; in many countries of Europe traditional puppet shows may still be discovered by the inquisitive traveller. In England we still have Punch and Judy, which happily shows no sign of dying out. But England, too, had until as recently as fifty years ago a rich tradition of marionette theatres. Artistically and technically they were, in their day, among the best in the world. Today not one of these traditional shows survives. There is, indeed, a new generation of puppeteers, in England as in many other countries, who are reinterpreting this ancient art in a contemporary idiom. It is good for any art to reflect its age. But it was also good, for a brief season, in so tangible a way, to bring the past to life.

How Long is
BASIN STREET?

FRED BASON

I WENT to the desk in the United States Embassy, gazed at the
pretty young lady for a moment, and took the plunge.
'Please will you tell me how long Basin Street is?' She said:
'I beg your pardon. Will you say that again?' 'It's ever so simple,'
I said; 'I'm Bason. I know how long I am—five foot five. I've come
nearly an hour's journey to find out how long is Basin Street.
You know of Basin Street? It's in New Orleans!'

She said: 'I've been here quite a long time and this is the oddest
piece of information I've been asked to locate. I will do my best
to help you. Will you wait five minutes?'

After a lot more than five minutes she returned. 'We seem to
be weak on books about New Orleans—and as for the length of
Basin Street we are quite unable to help you. We suggest you
write to New Orleans Public Library. We haven't the slightest
doubt that they can provide you with the required information
to the exact foot.' I departed.

Now you too may wonder why I wanted the answer to this
curious question, 'How long is Basin Street?' Let me tell you.

My dad told me, years ago, that in 1900 my grandfather had
owned about one-fifth of a notorious street in America and given
it all up because he'd turned to religion. I only remember my
grandfather as a deeply religious man. He lived at 10 Vowler
Street, Walworth. My father hadn't actually told me that the
street of which my grandfather had once owned a fifth was
Basin Street, but it didn't need Doctor Thorndyke or Mr.
Pinkerton to put two and two together and get four. Was it not
natural that I should like to know the length of Basin Street
and so know just how long one-fifth of it was? After all, with a
scrap of luck it could have been my dad's heritage, and he could

have left to me one-fifth of Basin Street, instead of 14s. 9d., a loud Victorian tie-pin, two books of how to bet on horses, and a useless collection of tools for repairing the harness of horses. (He was a saddler all his life.) These were my dear dad's total possessions after 73 years of living.

So I wrote to the President of the U.S.A., at The White House:

Dear Mister President,
I am an Honorary Member of The Mark Twain Society of U.S.A. and I have a certificate to prove it. There are only two other Honorary Members in England, John Masefield and Winston Churchill—so I am in quite exclusive company. . . . Now I need, Mr. President, a little information, and the American Embassy in London is unable to help me. It is a simple question: How long is Basin Street (which as you know is in New Orleans)?
I am, Sir, very cordially,
Fred Bason.

Whilst I was waiting for a reply to my letter to the President (for which I enclosed a new 15 cent stamp) I wrote to a London Public Library which prides itself on being able to answer any questions. The Librarian replied:

It appears that this street cannot be much longer than a couple of hundred yards or so. From the available map we do not find Basin Street marked at all, but a description tells us that it runs into Beauregard Square and as it does not show anywhere in the surrounding streets, Basin Street can only be a short alley. Hoping this satisfies your enquiry.

Well, blow me down! How on earth can a street two hundred yards in length be a short ALLEY? The whole street would rise up in arms if they heard that a Public Library called it an ALLEY.

Then I wrote to Mr. Smith, of Racine, who told me that as far as he knew Basin Street was 'not a very long street'. How long is 'long'? Next I wrote to Indianapolis Public Library. The head of their Social Sciences Division wrote:

Basin Street was one of the streets defining the boundaries of New Orleans 'red light' district in accordance with an ordinance to restrict vice, passed January 26th, 1897. The area was known as 'Storyville' after Alderman Story who sponsored the measure. Storyville was officially closed on October 10th, 1917, in response to a request from President Woodrow Wilson for the curbing of big city vice in wartime. The well-known song 'Basin Street Blues' was inspired by the colourful life of the quarter. Basin Street is often spoken of as the street on which Negro jazz originated.

Not a word about the *length* of the street. Now, had I known where to locate Louis Armstrong I am pretty sure my question would have gotten an answer, for he was not only raised in this street, learned to play the trumpet in this street, but had worked, played, slept and eaten—and lots of other things in Basin Street! But it is easier to write to the President of America than the President of the Trumpet. 'Satchmo' Armstrong always seems to be a most amiable Negro, but where to find him? In forty years I've interviewed some 8,000 celebrities, but I've never managed to get near Satchmo.

However, Duke University Library in North Carolina came up with a mine of information. They said my letter had caused a lot of laughter and they looked forward to helping me again. They quoted from Eleanor Early's *New Orleans Holiday*:

There were 38 blocks occupied solely by houses, restaurants, cabarets, saloons and cribs *all* devoted to vice and making a nice thing of it. . . . There were nearly 500 white girls and about half as many who were coloured.

They added that Herbert Asbury's *The French Quarter: An Informal History of New Orleans' Underworld* contains the following:

In 1899 when New Orleans had a population of about 285,000 [including my grandfather?] Mayor Flower reported that there were in Storyville 230 houses, 30 places of assignation and approximately 2,000 prostitutes.

Miss Early was correct. 750 prostitutes had grown to 2,000—making, as she said, 'a nice thing of it'. The wages of sin is *not* always death. The letter from Duke University Library continued:

For the number of brothels on Basin Street itself you could consult the directories of the Storyville District. The Blue Book, last of the series of directories, first issued about 1902, lists *all* prostitutes in Storyville, white and black; they were arranged by streets in some issues and alphabetically by names in others.

The letter contained the further information that Basin Street is shorter than it used to be—and it 'is a bit hard to tell where the street begins and ends'. So nobody knows.

The infuriating thing is that I once met a very distinguished man who was sure to have known—and I never asked him! In 1938 I appeared on the stage at the Trocadero Cinema, by the Elephant and Castle, in a show called 'In Town Tonight'. My stage act was to come out with a tray full of threepenny bits and defy any member of the audience to name a song or a tune I couldn't play on a piano at once. Since this was the second largest cinema in Europe it was no easy task. I played about eighty tunes correctly and failed only on three occasions. For my staggering performance I got a salary of 30s. per week.

However, on one memorable night the great Negro jazz pianist Art Tatum was encouraged to perform for five or six minutes (maybe just to show me how really to play jazz) during the show, and when his astounding performance was over he and I had a little chat. He said: 'Basin Street was gay, man—there was never any gayer. Hundreds of musicians got their break in the cribs and cabarets of Basin Street. No Basin Street, no Jazz. It's as simple as that. The Blues wasn't born there—but it was *improved* there. There are many forms of the Blues. The three-line verse is the common one—the repetition of the first line gives a singer time to invent a third line. And the Blues gave the player time to improvise on a basic harmonic structure.'

These were almost Art Tatum's words. I wrote them down at the time. He also talked of a traditional 12-bar structure and a Dominant seventh. I didn't know then, and I don't know now, what is a Subdominant third or a Dominant seventh. But Art Tatum knew exactly what he was talking about and I just listened. Then I created one of the most embarrassing situations of all my life. I held out my book and my pen and asked for his autograph. He put his hand into his waistcoat pocket and brought out a tiny box about two inches long and one inch wide. He opened the box and it was a rubber stamp pad with a tiny rubber stamp fascimile of his autograph.

He was utterly blind! I didn't know.

What a pity I didn't ask this great blind man how *long* Basin Street was! He'd have known. It was on the pianos of the brothels and honky-tonks of Storyville that early jazz techniques were being explored by such artists as 'Jelly Roll' Morton, who played the big white piano in Mahogany Hall, Lulu White's house. The brothels afforded wonderful opportunities for Negro musicians, especially for pianists. There was not a brothel of any importance in Storyville that did not have its 'professor' at the piano.

I can't think what my religious grandfather was doing there, though it might have suited his grandson Fred, who, after just two lessons of half an hour each, costing 1s. 6d. a lesson, from a Miss Smith at the age of ten, took to the piano as a duck takes to water. When I was sixteen I played the piano for a week in a Paris nightclub—played jazz; and no one taught me jazz.

It was a book called *Frenchmen Desire Good Children*, by John Chase, which finally cleared my grandfather's name. It seems that the Orleans Navigation Company cleared and widened the Carondelet canal, improved its turning basin, and dredged out Bayon St. John. A sum of $375,000 was spent on this work. But an ambitious plan to extend the canal from its turning basin, 'to the street which acquired the name of BASIN, to the street which acquired the name of Canal, and thence to the river, never came any closer to reality than a legendary legend on maps. . . .'

Thank you, John Chase, for chasing away my fears that my family had anything whatsoever to do with the name 'Basin Street'. Blame it on the Orleans Navigation Company. My grand-dad didn't get there till June 1898.

Altogether I spent over three months and wrote twenty-five letters to America trying to find out how long Basin Street was. Some of my correspondents gave me fascinating information. Basin Street, it seems, is no longer the street of sin; a government housing project stands where the red-light district used to be. Once a railway station stood there, but it was pulled down. All that remains of the orginal street is St. Louis Cemetery Number One. Jazz has moved out—and spread all over the world.

Yet, as a lady in New York City wrote to tell me, about the year 1900 Basin Street was quite a place. The mansions of sin were lavishly furnished in a violent and barbaric taste. They contained heavily carved plush-covered furniture, massive statuary, gaudy tapestries, leopard- and tiger-skin rugs, potted palms, and girls from all nations. Three celebrated madames controlled most of the Basin Street vice: 'Countess' Willie Piazza, Josie Arlington, and Lulu White. Collectively millions of dollars went through their hands—and they all died broke. The Countess had a piano in white that cost $200; at her death it made $1.25 at a public auction. It was badly out of tune. Lulu White's white grand piano realised $2.00. I don't know if Josie had a white piano in her palace, but there is a legend that a red light mysteriously shines from her tombstone on certain nights.

You may be interested to know that the area around Basin Street has produced four world boxing champions: Pete Herman, Tony Canzoneri, Willie Pastrano and Joe Brown. The longest fight in the history of boxing took place here in 1893 between Andy Bowen and Jack Burke. It took seven hours and fourteen minutes.

I could go on for a long time about the curiosities of Basin Street. 'Countess' Piazza was an octaroon and had a large musical box inside the mattress of her huge bed. Josie called her place 'Château Lobrano d'Arlington', and every room had a large mirror built in the ceiling.

But how *long* was Basin Street? In my room at 152 Westmoreland Road, S.E.17, I have a wonderful map of New Orleans. I've gazed at it for hours. It seems clear that Basin Street begins at the junction where there is the Bolivar Memorial or Monument (how did they come into the Basin story?) and ends somewhere around the cemetery. Perhaps it is now about six-tenths of a mile: in 1879 it might have been as much as one and a half miles.

If my grandfather in 1898 owned one-fifth, then he owned a considerable bit of property—cribs, bars, honky-tonks, or mansions with mirrors built into the ceilings and girls of all nations on the beds. But as the entire district was razed to the ground and re-created in 1940, there isn't anything his grandson can do about it—except, perhaps, to wait for the reply to that letter I wrote to the President of the United States and hope some Foundation will put up enough money to send me (with a tape measure) to complete my history of this famous street.

A CABBY
WITH
A CAMERA

PHOTOGRAPHS BY MAX GREEN

FIELD MARSHAL
SIR GEORGE STUART WHITE
V.C. G.C.B. O.M. G.C.S.I.
G.C.M.G. G.C.I.E. G.C.V.O.
BORN 1835

A cab driver like me sees all sorts of people grappling with the trials and thrills of their work. This chap on the left, now, he's obviously got to the top of the ladder—but still he has to take a back seat. The fellow on the right doesn't look much like Aladdin, but still he rubs away at his lamps. 'All I seem to get is sore hands,' he told me.

'Oh my!' said the coloured gentleman. 'Why are they all staring at me? All I want to do is to rest my weary legs.'

The most famous musicians in London? No, not the Philharmonic or the London Symphony Orchestra, but the 'Road Stars'. You'll see them most evenings round about Leicester Square. It isn't so often, though, that you see Dick Charlesworth and his City Gents rehearsing in the street. And nowadays the harpist is *quite* a rarity.

London's changing all the time, and by the time you look at this picture you won't see the vista I saw when I took it—one of the churches that luckily survived the Blitz, but which will soon be ringed round by other alien shapes. A bit surprising, too, is the view below. No, it's not the heart of the countryside, but a row of cottages in Mill Hill. Opposite—well, that needs no caption, does it? Nor does the picture overleaf—London's river.

Yes, all the world now recognises the face above that smiled so cheerily at me when he came to London. But you have to move around and keep your eyes open to spot such charming ladies as the artist below, or such splendid figures as the chap opposite—he's an accomplished musician, even though he doesn't know how to handle a razor.

There's nothing like the London parks. Athletic examples for the young. A blind eye for the amusements of those who are a shade older. And plenty of leaves for the oldies to sweep up in the autumn.

Traffic—don't talk about it! Underground garages is one solution, but the car on the left was looking for one too eagerly. I hope he didn't brush against the lady below. Personally I think we'd all do better if we went along with Neddy, above. My Mum always says, 'Once round the park does you the world of good.'

The Changing Face
of Horror

ALAN WALBANK

NEWSPAPER columnists, bishops, members of women's committees, schoolmasters, even university departments have for some time expressed concern that sex and violence, separately or combined, take an unduly prominent place in the reading matter both of the adult and the adolescent today. Lest we worry unduly, it has all happened before.

In an essay contributed to the first number of *Ainsworth's Magazine*, 1841, Martin Tupper buried the old promoters of sensation in the shape of the Gothic novel of mystery and horror. He declared the terrors of *Udolpho* as superannuated as the tremors of *Clarissa*.

Ghosts affright us not, who can ask with show of reason where they got their clothes from; skeletons are incidents that thrill no more in story since looked upon intrinsically as little better than phosphate of lime; for the Bleeding Nun school of tales we prescribe a styptic; for Red Rovers a course of solitary confinement and water gruel; for usurping uncles an amicable compromise to stay the ravages of Chancery.

Up to a point Tupper was right. The old type of Horrid Mystery had become *démodé*. In fact it began to go underground, into the basements and servants' quarters where last season's fashions or sensations still commanded an avid audience. Of such tales' continued popularity there the Mayhew brothers gave evidence in their *Adventures of a Lady in search of a good Servant*. For while pan bottoms burned out and dirty dishes filled the kitchen Betsy the cook was immersed in *The Castle Fiend*, *Heads of the Headless*, *The Black Pirate* or *The Maniac Father* as reprinted in the *Penny Sunday Times* and graced with a weekly engraving of some poor defenceless woman lying at the feet of a black-cloaked

o

brute, with her throat cut as wide open as a cheese, and weltering in a pool of ink.

Suchlike horrors were then with good reason being supplanted in upper-class readers' favour—except for traditional use in the Christmas Numbers. Instead of the stage effects of Teutonic romances terrors of actual life, from which few were wholly exempt, underlay Victorian tales of terror. The life, however, was not of the sort recognised in broad day: for which the early Victorian ethos was to blame. This required that much of life should be neither seen, discussed nor thought of: not only the grosser things but many ordinary facts of existence were draped, like table legs, or covered, like tea-pot spouts. Excessive prudery and religious terrorism, together with the refusal of a successful middle class to face the evil beside their path, paved the way to a peculiar hell of the imagination. From this underworld of repression there was an uprush of sinister emanations, finding relief in a spate of sensational tales and novels. The most widespread and debasing form of evil towards which respectable Victorians turned a blind eye was pauperdom and crime. Its extent and depth being a result of the *laissez faire* machine system, the uprooting of rural families and the forced urbanisation wherein middle-class prosperity was based, there was naturally an unwillingness to look such facts full in the face. At the same time nervous fears mounted of some violent outbreak from these lower regions.

Oliver Twist marks a turning point in themes of terror. A London alderman publicly declared that Jacob's Island as described by Dickens did not exist and never had existed. It was part of Dickens's purpose, at risk of shocking those who expected crime to be presented in terms of *The Beggar's Opera*, to set down what he himself had witnessed and knew to be the truth. Sikes's unrelieved brutality, the foul and frowzy company of Fagin's thieves, the wretched Nancy's life squandered in the streets and stews, were Dickens's answer to the romances of Lytton. The ugliness of their story set beside the ideal domesticity of the Maylies added its extra horror, for none who watched the struggles of an innocent orphan, trapped in that nightmare world that lay just round the corner, could do so without recognising the implication, while the insistent strokes of Dickens's revelation of poverty and vice were inescapable. Furthermore the whole cause of Oliver's 'adventures', money left to an illegitimate child and a step-brother's plot to retain it, cut deep into the middle-class conscience.

Twenty years later Dickens was to reopen the crack that ran between respectability's façade and the structure supporting it, in *Great Expectations*. Here awareness of the criminal world came accidentally to Pip, the blacksmith's apprentice, forced to fetch food and a file to the convict hiding in the graveyard. This unpleasant knowledge was put aside, however, as he learned the ways of Satis House and met its beautiful ward Estella, and when, in hopes of becoming her match, he was living as a gentleman on his surprise allowance in London. How hypocritical the meeting there with the honest blacksmith made him, after money and its pretensions had become the measure of worth! A first appalling blow, when the convict Magwitch turned out to be his benefactor and his allowance to have come from earnings in a penal settlement, only paved the way for worse. Estella, too, turned out to have a tainted past, being the daughter of both a criminal and a murderess. All Pip's hopes of so-called gentility crumbled away. He was able to purge his error only in the fire of his terrible escape from death in the old sluice-house on the flats, by sharing the ordeal of life-and-death pursuit on the river and the suffering of Magwitch in the prison hospital.

For the middle-class public these books held more than mere sensation—the vicarious and half-pleasurable response to menace. They allowed secret fears to be shared and guilt confessed. The reader at once suffered and was relieved of a burden, such a burden as perhaps prompted Elizabeth Barrett Browning to write her over-charged drama of a ruined girl's life among the slums of London and Paris in *Aurora Leigh*.

A more obvious source of terror writing connected with the social conditions of the period from the 'forties to the 'seventies is undetected murder. In his *Cornhill* article, 'On being found out', Thackeray playfully assumed that hundreds of murders were committed without anyone being the wiser, pretending that he himself knew of one or two almost infalliable methods. He only withheld them lest some monster might make away with his wife. In the same vein James Payn once hazarded a guess that one person in every five hundred was an undiscovered murderer.

The publication, in 1829, of the memoirs of Vidocq, founder of the Service de Sûreté of Paris, and the dubious writings of his rival and successor Cocu-Lacour, drew increased attention to cases of violence and to the battles of wit waged, often in the heart of the underworld, before their equally violent punishment.

Moreover the whole nation had been startled and fascinated by three extraordinary cases—that of Palmer the poisoner in 1856, of Madeleine Smith, of whom it was finally 'not proven' that she had put arsenic in her lover's chocolate in 1857, and of Constance Kent in 1860. This well-bred girl cut her half-brother's throat by way of expressing disapproval of step-mothers and second marriages, and then allowed her father and a nurse to be suspected of the crime. The detective investigating this affair appeared thinly disguised in Dickens's articles and inspired Wilkie Collins to originate a new species in English fiction with his Sergeant Cuff of *The Moonstone*. So, apart from being a source of nervous apprehension and an unrivalled news item, in times of comparative peace and when sex was virtually debarred murder opened a new field for the professional writer. Further involuntary interest sprang from the latent sympathy felt for the rebel, whether against society, moral conventions or domestic tyranny, who gave vent in murder to all the suppressed violence of both his own and his audience's private state.

Against the tyranny of the head of the family and the code of behaviour he upheld there was in reality little chance to rebel without disaster. A spirited daughter setting her heart on the wrong suitor might turn into a disappointed old maid, a too outspoken wife or overbold son by attempting independence might queer his or her whole future; yet, so long as the law gave a husband undisputed right over his wife's property and custom made him controller of the family purse, they had no choice but submission to his will.

As a statement of family power Le Fanu's *Uncle Silas* may come perilously near the grotesque, but it never releases the reader from its psychological grip. At the death of her father, a wealthy recluse and disciple of Swedenborg, his seventeen-year-old daughter Maud is placed until her coming of age under the authority of her uncle, Silas Ruthyn of Bartram-Hough, and a large fortune is bequeathed to her in trust. Silas, invalidish, in debt, socially ostracised, queerly religious, plans to marry his degenerate son to Maud and so acquire complete control. From the time when she enters Bartram-Hough, increasing pressure is put upon Maud's helplessness and sensitive apprehension. The very atmosphere of the long galleries and gloomy courtyard, the perfumes, the ether and laudanum of her uncle's room, his mesmeric personality, are enough to soften resistance: they are reinforced by the malignant attentions of a foreign governess.

When 'fair' means seem slow in inducing her submission the design of seizing all by murder supervenes. Maud, the perfect adolescent reagent to terror, moves towards its consummation. For the crisis of this plan Le Fanu employs all the circumstantial realism of a police report.

The murderer drew from his pocket an instrument which I saw distinctly against the faint moonlight—a hammer, one end of which had been beaten out into a longish tapering spike, with a handle something longer than usual. . . . Suddenly but softly he laid, as it seemed to me, his left hand over her face, and nearly at the same instant there came a scrunching blow: an unnatural shriek, beginning small and swelling for two or three seconds into a yell, such as are imagined in haunted houses, accompanied by a convulsive sound, as of the motion of running, and the arms drumming on the bed; and then another blow—and with a horrid gasp he recoiled a step or two, and stood perfectly still. I heard a horrible tremor quivering through the joints and curtains of the bedstead—the convulsions of the murdered woman. It was a dreadful sound, like the shaking of a tree and rustling of leaves. Then once more he stepped to the side of the bed, and I heard another of those horrid blows—and silence—and another—and more silence—and the diabolical surgery was ended.

But, in keeping with his macabre design, it is the intended victim who becomes the paralysed spectator of this murder, and the grim governess its actual subject. So while Maud feels and distils its horror to the full, the pressure put upon the reader by the story's masterly twists and prolonged suspense bursts not in tragedy, but in sense of relief.

The 'persecuted woman' theme, with implied suffering or actual agony inflicted on the shattered nerves or shaken brain of a defenceless girl, persistently crops up in fiction from the time of *Pamela* and *Clarissa* to that of Faulkner's *Sanctuary* and its derivative, *No Orchids for Miss Blandish*. With the Victorians it merely changed direction.

Instead of seduction or rape, money now became the prime object, while the relationship became a family one, paternal or marital, instead of the simpler one between male and female. The classic handling of the theme of terror based on marital persecution came from Collins. Again it is noteworthy that the crux of the plot in *The Woman in White* derived from an account of a real French lawsuit casually picked up on a Paris stall. Collins significantly changed the persons there involved from brother and sister to husband and wife. In essentials the plan remained the same: to make the lady disappear after obtaining possession of her wealth.

Following closely on *The Woman in White* came *Lady Audley's Secret*, to make man pay with a vengeance. The golden-haired beauty with the face of an angel could look on while her first husband fell down a well, and calmly leave him there to an assumed death. In her subsequent career Lady Audley apparently had no qualms, except lest she should be found out. So, when a relative of her second husband became too inquisitive, she double-locked his bedroom door and then set fire to the inn in which he was sleeping. For the scene of this midnight conflagration Miss Braddon employed exceptionally vivid and lingering description, and, both with Victorian mothers and daughters, the story proved a phenomenal success. Vicariously it afforded a complete and violent turning of the domestic tables.

For the authoress this was a fateful beginning. Public demand led Miss Braddon to write to the same pattern for most of her career. Later her popular mixture included excursions into high life and low life, the night haunts of Paris and the London burlesque theatre, while amateur detection also played its part. But, true to the poles of Victorian interest, which, it has been remarked, was drawn equally to fictional crime and to accounts of fatal accidents, she continued liberally to produce the suburban murder. On occasion, as in *Wyllard's Weird*, a railway accident might be included too. In one of her later books, however, occurs a sign of something beyond the recognised themes and motives. In *Thou Art the Man* an epileptic subject, Brandon Mountford, suddenly finds that his disease has become a homicidal instinct,[1] and so renounces the woman he loves in fear of yielding to a mad impulse to murder her. Shortly afterwards her adopted sister Marie, who has accidentally revealed a jealous love for the same man, is found by him dead in the shrubbery. Stumbling over the body he starts to his knees with a shriek of horror.

> The hand that had been lying on her breast was wet and dabbled with blood. He knew the touch of that. For the hunter and the dweller in the wilderness there could be no uncertainty as to that thick and viscous fluid which covered his clammy fingers and trickled about his wrist.

The knife that has cut Marie's throat is his and the case seems all too clear. . . . In the sequel, however, a death-bed confession reveals that Brandon's fears and his subsequent flight from justice were both unnecessary. Not he, but another man whose passionate love Marie had rejected with loathing, was the murderer in the shrubbery. Brandon's fit and the chance use of his knife had obscured this, wrongly linking cause and effect. Nevertheless Miss Braddon's story rightly linked with the Victorian terror theme its third main element, fear of sex.

To exhibit the actual course of things in a story of love, whether lawless or lawful, was, as Gissing observed, utterly forbidden by the Victorian conventions. On the other hand a novelist might indulge in ghastly bloodshed to any extent of which his stomach was capable. Gore was perfectly decent, but the secrets of passion too shameful even to whisper. As one result of this, passion in fiction appears allied with or translated into terms of bloodshed to a remarkable extent. The generation that read of Porphyria strangled by her lover with her own yellow tresses, in Browning's 1845 volume, found in killing a special excitement.[2] It might be equated according to

---

1 A similar case was tried at the Old Bailey nine years before. A convicted murderer was reprieved after having a fit.

2 Again, Rossetti found a special attraction in employing Madeline Smith, lately tried for murder, as a model.

circumstances with sexual possession or with its frustration. Sikes's killing of Nancy is in the novel the logical outcome of their anti-social alliance, as between burglar and prostitute. But Dickens's rendering of the scene in his last public readings, with so horrific an effect that a dozen or more women had to be carried out in faints, seems to have afforded him both dramatic outlet for the failure of his own marriage and a compensatory sense of dominance over woman. The murder of Porphyria springs from awareness of incomplete sexual fulfilment, followed by an urge to destroy for others what the lover cannot have for himself. This negation may be rooted in the conflict between normal desire and the period decorum, heightened by con-sciousness of the struggle between the sexes. At a lower social level conflict of another sort, that between the excessive demands made on man by the machine and his natural instincts, leads to the same symbolic result. In Zola's bloodshot novel *La Bête Humaine* the zealous engine driver, for whom his locomotive almost usurps the position of mistress, finds he can only kill when he should love: terror opens on the dark sexual chasm leading to destruction not creation of life. The author, it will be remarked, conveys an acute sense of pleasure in his climactic scene of slaughter, set in the red-papered, red-curtained bed-room, and after it the murderer feels pride and gratification of his male sovereignty.

For the literary source of the peculiar sex-murder motif in Victorian fiction one must look further afield. Publication in the 'forties of the stories of Edgar Allan Poe had done more than introduce the art of detection into literature: it had opened for writers the door of abnormal psychology. Poe and his fellow countryman, Hawthorne, were both familiars of dark ideas in an era of Puritan morality. While the author of *The Scarlet Letter*, however, of *Ethan Brand* and *The House of the Seven Gables*, broods over the mystery of sin and its persisting curse in a detached, even delicate way:

> A furtive soul whose dark romance
> By ghostly door and haunted stair,
> Explored the dusty human heart
> And the forgotten garrets there—

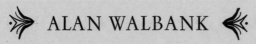

Poe, on the other hand, probes harshly and curiously into the criminal psyche and exploits all its most hideous terrors. He selects the most bizarre crimes, peers into the recesses of conscience and excludes no device for intensifying the reader's reaction. In 'The Tell-tale Heart', for example, the suspense as the murderer inch by inch projects the beam of his dark lantern and malevolent eye upon his bed-fast victim, deliberately prolonging his death agony, becomes barely tolerable. Poe's morbid fantasies have a specially compulsive force. Who could fail to recognise the significance of 'William Wilson', that frantic double personality in whom the entanglement and conflict of bad with good eventually produces self-murder: or of 'Ligeia', a woman whose vehement response to passion extends after death through the man she had loved to bring her successor's life to a sudden, alarming end? Her simulacrum appears to claim him from the very corpse of the wife he watches. D. H. Lawrence rightly recognised here the thirst for unrealisable love, love pushed to an extreme where the only question becomes which of the lovers shall destroy the other first. When, in 'The Black Cat', an imp of perversity born of intemperance leads its subject to torture his household animals, to kill his wife who dares to interfere, and afterwards in manic hallucination to betray his own crime, one feels oneself on familiar period and domestic ground. Finally, beneath its Gothic trappings, the House of Usher displays a symbolic split in its fabric, while consciousness of social futility and decay cause the brother and sister within to clasp each other in a death embrace.

The British Victorian novelists handled such themes in a different way, involving the symbolism more closely with situations in real life and implanting the horrors in more ordinary backgrounds. For sequel to 'Ligeia' one turns to *Wuthering Heights,* where, even in her opened coffin, Heathcliff asserts his love for the Catherine who has married another, and destroys that rival's happiness as his is destroyed by her. After death the country folk say he still haunts their old place of meeting. The revulsion from life and death-wish at work in the House of Usher finds its parallel in Satis House. Here, in *Great Expectations*, the frustrated and obsessed Miss Havisham not only shuts herself up amid rotting relics from her unfulfilled bridal day, halting time until her end shall come, but to be avenged on life she brings up Estella, her ward, to torment and never satisfy the hearts of men who desire her. Dickens, as will appear later, also reopened the case of 'William Wilson' and was unable to close it. Finally, from 'The Black Cat' one passes straight to Le Fanu's black monkey in 'Green Tea'. When that visitant from the unchaste subconscious of a pious and handsome bachelor begins to thwart him in his clerical observances, urges him to injure his fellows, tempts him to throw himself down a mine-shaft before his niece's eyes, and at length leads to his frightful suicide, there, unmistakably, are the signs of sex denied or gone wrong, of disturbances at the very fount of the normal will to live.

Impulses suppressed or confined in the ordinary course of life naturally find outlet in other ways. Relationships between the opposite sexes being hedged in with restrictions, that between members of the same sex became charged with a higher emotional current. At some point, not necessarily an extreme one, guilty fear followed. It was partly assuaged when expression was found by way of fantasy for emotional situations of the type usually excluded from Victorian reading. Use of the older 'horrid mystery' setting, as in Le Fanu's 'Carmilla', might act as camouflage but it was quite transparent. The situation here involves a young girl, living alone except for her father in a typical Gothic castle deep in the forest, who acquires through a travelling accident a beautiful female companion. The new-comer's languid charm and brilliant appearance compel the girl's admiration.

Sometimes my strange and beautiful companion would take my hand and hold it with fond pressure, renewed again and again, blushing softly and breathing so fast that her dress rose and fell with the tumultuous respiration. It was like the ardour of a lover. With gloating eyes she drew me to her, and her hot lips travelled along my cheeks in kisses. She would whisper, almost in sobs, 'You are mine, you shall be mine, you and I are one for ever.'

Pleasurable excitement is aroused in the girl at first, gradually to be mingled with fear and disgust, as the stranger's insistent attentions increase. The reader's sensations are lengthily indulged before the truth of this Lesbian relationship comes out. For in her sleep a feeling as if warm lips kiss her, longer and more lovingly as they reach her throat, fixes itself in a convulsive caress under which the girl faints. Then the horror attendant on their relationship becomes clear. Her companion is indeed a vampire, whose passion cannot be satiated until it has drained the very life-blood of its victim. The moral and the social dangers illumined are obvious. Le Fanu was writing at a time when, apart from the restrictive code of behaviour, there was a marked preponderance of young women over the young men available as husbands (a situation aggravated by losses in the Crimean War) and when the alternative outlet of a career was hardly feasible for respectable middle-class girls. His own attitude remains ambivalent, as he allows Carmilla at the start to exact sympathy and consent, and then protracts her illicit enjoyment with the refinement of an epicure.

There are many minor pieces and incidents in the works of writers less committed to the dark side of life that supply comment on these guilty fears and impulses. Among her *Tales for Christmas Eve* published in 1873 Rhoda Broughton, a niece of Le Fanu, includes a particularly shocking double murder of a late married husband and wife. The wife's girlhood friend, still a spinster, has just been on a visit and given her vain forewarning of tragedy. In a dream she has heard sounds of muffled struggling in their bedroom and a strangled cry: on her venturing at last to look in 'it seemed as if that bed were only one horrible sheet of crimson'. The throats of man and wife had huge, yawning gashes, the husband's *grey* hair was all reddened and stained. Then in a mirror she saw a figure with a red, wet sickle in his hand walking across the room. The dream, of course, has a matter-of-fact sequel, but its symbolism remains unimpaired.

To dwell on the forbidden, investing it with the trappings of terror, was a typical Victorian trait. Both Collins and Dickens made the bed the centrepiece of several stories—'The Double-bedded Room', 'The Bride's Chamber', 'A Terribly Strange Bed'. In view of their joint sprees on the continent some more personal significance may have attached to the last tale. Here the valanced and curtained four-poster is used to suffocate between heavy mattresses a wealthy British visitor to a Paris gambling house. Even in the innocuous family novels of Mrs Henry Wood there is some occasion for surprise if death imagery be taken as a reflex of repression. Readers of *The Shadow of Ashlydyat*, for instance, wallowed in the oppressive anguish of four death-bed scenes including that of the heroine, and a whole chapter per decease was no unusual ration.

The first and perhaps the richest material for studies in the period's thanatosis, however, was supplied by Samuel Warren, whose passages from *The Diary of a Late Physician*, published in *Blackwood's Magazine* between 1830 and 1837, enjoyed wide circulation in three-volume form. The whole purpose of this work was to exhibit death-beds—of baronet's bride and prostitute, forger and profligate, pugilist and beautiful consumptive—and so to illustrate the practical working of virtues and vices. Warren did so with a wealth of circumstantial detail and lingering accounts of his unhappy subjects and their agonies, so that his choice of scenes, hitherto kept from public observation, were, in the words of the American editor, 'well calculated to furnish both instruction and amusement'.

The principal sources of terror so far considered, social fears and guilt, family tyranny and violence, sex repression and distortion, were deeply founded in the Victorian psyche. Their expression in fiction, if not always bringing relief, at least brought into daylight some of the causes man had to fear himself, while the general craving for these homoeopathic horrors was perhaps an instinctive desire to be inoculated against the real thing. In his recollections Edmund Yates, for instance, records the murder tales current in his youth and their fascination: especially that of the killer who cut up the body of his victim, carrying the head wrapped up in a handkerchief on his knees in the omnibus, and who was supposed to have nearly fainted with fright when, on asking the conductor the fare, the man replied: 'Sixpence a *head.*' To introduce humour into murder is another way of reducing its actual terror. Less deeply rooted but quite as alarming elements also deserve notice. The abuse of private asylums, prominent in *The Woman in White*, was thoroughly ventilated in Charles Reade's *Hard Cash* (1863). A more remarkable source of terror theme was thuggee.

During the 'thirties the British government in India had had considerable trouble in putting down a brotherhood of professional stranglers or thugs, and two books by retired officers had been written about them. Eugene Sue had then introduced a thug into European circles in his *Wandering Jew*, and a garrotting epidemic in London during the 'fifties caused the topic to be reopened. In *The Moonstone* Collins brought into the background of ordinary British life a band of Hindu devotees who committed a secret murder: Dickens now decided to go one better with *Edwin Drood*. John Jasper, cathedral choirmaster and opium addict, was to murder Drood Hindu fashion, with the long scarf he wore round his neck. Like Poe's William Wilson, Jasper is a divided personality and seems to symbolise the middle-class moral split, when the left hand of Christian 'love thy neighbour' tradition refuses to acknowledge what the right hand of *laissez-faire* capitalism is doing. Not only is Jasper conversant with thuggee and opium (a traffic needing public ventilation at that time), he is also a hypnotist.

Again, theories of mesmerism or electro-biology had already been elaborated, by Bulwer Lytton in *The Haunters and the Haunted, or The House and the Brain*, and in 'A Strange Story', which appeared in *All the Year Round* under Dickens's editorship. The latter, taking advantage of a growing craze for psychical research, now brought in the whole repertory of Mesmer's feats and practices. The insistent keynote of the piano and the swelling note of the organ that so frighten Rosa, shrinking object of Jasper's attentions, remind us of the contemporary belief that hypnotic influence could be projected by sound alone. And for evidence of the public alarm attaching to this pseudo-science, even without the addition of thuggee, one need look no further than to present-day enquiries about stage hypnotism and its after effects. Again no doubt the substitute fears of Edwin Drood served to relieve a real dread.

After the 'sixties writing about crime and detection departed more and more from what may be termed 'criticism of life' and developed, in the hands of the better practitioners, into a species of logical exercise. The cult of the detective as a type of omniscient superman became more marked: so much so that an Oxford Professor of Poetry has seen in him a popular substitute for the Deity during an era of declining religious faith, with the murderer, of course, as scapegoat. On the lower level police 'revelations' were constantly appearing, frequently in yellow-back form. One of the early cheap libraries of popular authors, for instance, listed *Curiosities of Detection, Secret Police, The French Detective Officer's Adventures, Irish Police Officer* and appropriately *Recollections of Botany Bay*: another list provided the more titillating *Experiences of the Lady Detective*. If the detective tale suggested a new embodiment of superhuman power, the romance of the police force may be regarded as typifying the romance of common man striving always for order out of chaos, or for stability in an age of social unrest. At all events, public taste, stimulated by translation of the famous *L'Affaire Lerouge* by the father of French detective fiction Emile Gaboriau, exhibited a voracious craving for this novel form. It would be easier to believe that in the crime story readers fulfilled the two sides of their own natures so often in conflict: that of the rebel and wrongdoer, and of the instrument of justice and self-punishment. Did the figure of the policeman, with restraining hand on the shoulder, represent anything more than conscience?

One is reminded here of a remark by Collins: 'I am subject to a curious ghostly influence, having often the idea that someone is standing behind me.' Allowing for the nervous state induced by his laudanum habit and domestic complications, Collins in these words seems to have placed an unerring finger on the general symptoms of the age. Who else was that 'someone' than the ambivalent shadow of the lurking tempter and the moral censor by which the whole of middle-class society was haunted? It was being pursued, in fact, by the terrors which Tupper had believed decently buried, in new, more insidious shape: their dwelling place not a Gothic ruin now, but the ordinary suburban household. Smothered in creepers and shrubberies outside, in curtains, canopies and portières within, the furniture muffled as though hiding from itself, the house

[238]

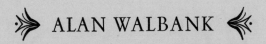

too had become a source of terror—for what it knew and tried to conceal, for all its family secrets, its tyrannies and impotent fantasies, its desperate attempts to hush up the facts.

Between late Victorian days and our own, themes of violence, horror and sex have certainly not abated in popularity, either for the bookstalls, films of the 'blondes, blood and beatings' type or for TV programmes. But they have changed: and not only from the impact of two world wars, gangsterdom, genocide, space travel and Freud, with their concomitant madness, guilt and mass despair. Like almost everything else such themes have succumbed to specialisation.

Just as 'detection stories' proper have come via the 'fair-play' type of plot from *Sherlock Holmes, Father Brown,* Austin Freeman, Father Ronald Knox to Agatha Christie, Dorothy Sayers and 'Nicholas Blake', presenting the logical solution of fairly stated problems but involving more and more esoteric knowledge: so 'crime stories' or psychological studies of the criminal's mind have come to Simenon and his imitators, where the crime itself is quite summarily treated. What may be termed 'thrillers', where criminological problems are often revealed by coincidence or accident, have reached their apogee so far with James Bond, 'spy stories' as a class with John le Carré. A whole genre of horror themes have stemmed from H. G. Wells's *The Island of Dr. Moreau* and the alarming libido shown at work in *Dr Jekyll and Mr Hyde.* Any bookstall today will show how 'shockers' of sex and violence, science and sadism, mystery and monsters from the subconscious have proliferated in complete paperback series and syndicates of such pulp writers as 'Hank Janson'. *Backlash of Infamy* is a typical title: 'genius, louse, rapist and four people wanted him dead' reads the blurb.

Viewed in relation to the neuroses of their times—the new fears of police states, atomic warfare, biological disaster, the playing with edged tools of scientific knowledge—such publications offer an almost surrealist expression of the collective psyche of the period. They give overt recognition to ideas so readily driven underground. And partly, perhaps, by their homoeopathic horrors they afford a layer of protection against the real thing.

LADIES AT SEA

Words & Pictures chosen by
CHARLES GIBBS-SMITH

She was taken down to Cowes secretly, and suddenly dashed out among the assembled ships at what was then the astounding speed of 34½ knots. Naturally she caused a great sensation.

—*Encyclopaedia Britannica*

The form of the under-water body was generally taken from designs which had already proved satisfactory; but the alterations in upper works produced marked differences in appearance.

—G. S. L. CLOWES: *Sailing Ships*

Quite large ships are launched broadside on. This often provides a startling spectacle, the ship being literally dropped bodily over the quay wall into the water, creating a flurry of waves and foam.

—J. S. REDSHAW: *Ships*

After the rendezvous, I could wait no longer to see the *Bathyscaphe*. . . .
I swam round the submerged machine and found her floating well,
with no gas leaks. —J. Y. COUSTEAU: *The Silent World*

The calculations involved in working out the suitability of hull form may well be imagined. Comprehensive tests are carried out in the tanks, and the behaviour of the model is accurately recorded by instruments of remarkable ingenuity.

—P. DUFF: *British Ships and Shipping*

Going afloat takes many forms besides the lift and surge of a boat under sail.

—*Weekend Telegraph*

A number of fishes produce sounds, some by means of the swim-bladder, others by the movement of parts of the skeleton against each other. We know nothing of the significance of these noises.

—*Chambers's Encyclopaedia*

The sea-shore is the haunt of a rich and varied collection . . . and has, on account of its unique position at the junction of sea and land, an interest altogether out of proportion to its area.

—RUSSELL AND YONGE: *The Seas*

The Captain was trying to pick out a small island . . . When he managed to focus on the island, he was astonished to find that it was something quite different, . . . About a quarter of an hour later, the object again rose slowly out of the sea.

—C. BOWEN, in *Flying Saucer Review*

The duties of steward vary according to
the description of merchant or passenger
vessel. . . . No seamanship is expected of him.
—W. S. LINDSAY: *History of Merchant Shipping*

It is an Automa, runnes under water,
With a snug nose, and has a nimble taile
Made like an auger, with which taile she wrigles
Betwixt the coasts of a ship, and sinks it streight.
　　　　　　—BEN JONSON: *The Staple Newes*

Missile away!... It was successful, and
so was that of the second mock missile.
　　　　　　—*National Geographic Magazine*

you are particularly requested not to speak to the Woman at the Wheel

The custom of carrying a certain number of the seamen's wives to sea, appears to have prevailed all through the eighteenth century.

—C. N. ROBINSON:
The British Fleet

She was replete with pleasantly full curves. The bow was rather high and the stern piece much like a segment of a circle; the poop narrow, with bulging quarters, and she had a full sweeping steer.

—H. B. CULVER: *The Book of Ships*

JETSAM—goods or other things which, having been cast over board in a storm, or after shipwreck, are thrown upon the shore, and belong to the lord admiral.   —JOHNSON's *Dictionary*

Built of soft wood, she has a full bottom and water-tight compart-
ments. . . . These craft, owing to their light draught and bulky top-
hamper, are not much good going to windward.

—E. K. CHATTERTON: *Sailing Ships*

Besides her alternative systems o
propulsion, a great advance was th
use of planes which could be incline
to the horizontal, by means of which
she could dive and rise while unde
way.
—*Science Museum*
Catalogue of Water Transpo